# METAPHYSICAL GRAFFITI

Feb 2019

# METAPHYSICAL GRAFFITI

## ROCK 'N' ROLL
## AND THE MEANING OF LIFE

## SETH KAUFMAN

OR Books
New York · London

All rights information: rights@orbooks.com
Visit our website at www.orbooks.com

First trade printing 2019

"In My 'Glee' Tribute to Lou Reed Episode" first appeared in newyorker.com.

Library of Congress Cataloging-in-Publication Data: A catalog record for this book is available from the Library of Congress.

British Library Cataloging in Publication Data: A catalog record for this book is available from the British Library.

Typeset by Lapiz Digital Services.

Published for the book trade by OR Books in partnership with Counterpoint Press. Distributed to the trade by Publishers Group West.

paperback ISBN 978-1-949017-08-3 • ebook ISBN 978-1-949017-09-0

This is for Daniel Blackman,
Jamie Pallot, Mitch Rosen, Dan Roth
and Seth Walter. Rock stars all.

# CONTENTS

# AN ACOUSTIC INTRO

THE ANNE AND BERNARD SPITZER HALL OF HUMAN ORIGINS IN the American Museum of Natural History in New York City gives visitors an overview of millions of years of human history. It's a slick and informative exhibit about our ancestors and evolution. Among the highlights on display, you can see Lucy, the finest 2-to-4 million-year-old hominid specimen in existence.

The exhibit has a small display about music, which of course is very much part of the human experience, and unique to the species. Birds aren't "singing" because they are happy. They make sounds that may sound like music at times, but those sounds are not music; no, those sounds are the result of an ingrained, inherited reflex.

A section in the music display is titled HOW AND WHY DID MUSIC ORIGINATE? It speculates on a number of possible social functions of music, noting it could have been "used for courtship, territorial claims, and uniting social groups." And it ends with this: "Whatever its original uses, music is now present in every human culture, implying that a biological capacity for music evolved early in our species' history."

I love this sign because, in a world-class museum that is dedicated to studying, cataloging, displaying and explaining so much of the natural world, what this sign really says is: *Nobody knows when or why music first started, but we think it must be goddamn important.*

So music, it turns out, is a bigger black hole than a black hole itself. I'm not kidding: Go to New York's Rose Center for Earth and Space, right next door to the Museum of Natural History, and you will see that we know far more about the origins and the structure of the universe than we do about the origins of music. There's even a super-cool four-minute movie exhibit in a concave theater about the Big Bang. It's a bit more elaborate than three or four speculative paragraphs about the origins of music at Spitzer Hall.

This makes sense. The first music left no swirling cosmos to measure, no rate of expansion, no bones to examine, no sheet music, no instruments. There was no iPhone to capture the first handclap, the first drumbeat, or the first harmony, never mind the first song—all those initial sounds have vanished. Perhaps one day scientists will be able to somehow capture the ancient sound waves of Lucy singing in Kenya to her hominid clan. But until those long-vanished waves are retrieved—which seems like a plot from an unwritten Michael Crichton novel—we are clueless.

The other reason I love the sign at Spitzer Hall is that I've been asking myself why music exists and what its purpose is ever since I heard "Mr. Roboto," a ridiculous song by Styx, in the mid-1980s. And the museum answer—or non-answer—may be frustrating at first, but I also find it empowering. If there's no answer to the Biggest Question—"Why music?"—and all the smartest guys in the museum have to work with is speculation, then the other Big Questions that consume us about music and music culture—Beatles or Stones? Does Rush Suck?—seem equally open to debate and speculation, and perhaps, in relative terms, are potentially answerable.

*Metaphysical Graffiti* tackles some of the most important and contentious Big Questions about music, specifically rock and pop music, and about those who listen to it. The BQ's may seem inane to someone who doesn't see the importance or the difficulty of picking the Beatles over the Stones or the Stones over the Beatles. Questioning the authenticity of Billy Joel may seem absurd to someone who doesn't care about Billy Joel in the first place, or (shudder!) loves him unquestioningly, or doesn't care about why they shouldn't care about Billy Joel. But these are not just stupid/funny rockhead questions to inspire comic debate—although they are that, too. They are also questions that, if we take them seriously, force us to look deeper into the relationship between music and our lives, and how we are shaped and how music is shaped.

In the end, I hope this book will provide some insight into difficult questions. Not to the original "Why music?" question—which no doubt is rooted in strengthening communal bonding among hunter-gatherers, finding the perfect mate, or some other very sensible social evolutionary reason. But answers to the meaning of music for each of us, and answers to the questions that music inspires. Ultimately, music is fascinating not just because of the complexity of notes or its sophisticated meter or its moving lyrics, but because of its many mystical powers to move us and consume us, to make us want to dance, to listen to it over and over again, or rush to turn it off, or analyze it, feel it, react to it, judge it, bathe in it or reject it, and then re-engage with it all over again.

And then, in a perfect world, find somebody you can argue with about it.

# BEATLES OR STONES? OR THE QUESTION OF IDENTITY

FOR MANY, THE ALL-ENCOMPASSING QUESTION "BEATLES OR Stones?" is instantly taken as shorthand for the question "Which band do you like better?"

For others, it's interpreted as a trick question, and the answer, of course, is Led Zeppelin.

One of the intriguing aspects of this question is that it isn't even a complete question. Beatles or Stones *what*? We are asked to choose, but not told, exactly, what it is we are choosing. A band? The band's music? The songs? The band's fashion sense?

The open-endedness of "Beatles or Stones?" brings us to the question of how we define rock bands—what they mean to us. When we think about the Beatles or Rolling Stones, there are an infinite amount of properties to focus on. We might think about how cool Keith Richards looks casually jabbing and flailing at one of his low-slung Fender Telecasters, or how outrageously entertaining Mick Jagger is performing his signature spastic funky-chicken moves up on stage. We remember the sight of John, Paul, George and Ringo running for their lives in *A Hard Day's Night*. We marvel at the entrancing, all-encompassing soundscape, narrative, poetry and truth that is found in both "A Day in the Life" and, on a different level, "She Loves You." We recall the irresistibly infectious opening of the Stones' "Honky Tonk Women," which tattoos itself on your brain with a cowbell-and-drums hook like no other in the history of recorded music. We remember studying the cover of the Beatles' *Abbey Road* for hours, and we remember laughing at the adolescent conceptual comedy of the Stones' infamous *Sticky Fingers* album cover, designed by Andy Warhol, that featured an actual working zipper embedded on the photo of a bulging male crotch.

The attributes and associations with both bands are exponential. Each record cover, each song, every lyric, every riff, every solo, every beat, all the videos (yes, the Beatles had videos prior to the dubious "Free as a Bird;" *Magical Mystery Tour* is basically one giant promotional film, made in 1967, 14 years before the launch of MTV), all the concerts, all the drugs you did while listening to the music, all the car rides with the radio on, all the friends and lovers who listened to them with you, all the movies and documentaries, all the books, all the posters (and the patches—don't forget the iron-on patches on your denim jacket, or your dad's or grandfather's denim jacket circa 1973)— the list goes on and on.

These very personal associations make the answer to "Beatles or Stones?" extremely hard to calculate, especially if you are a fan of both groups.

But let's try to do the math. In an insane attempt to rationally, somewhat objectively settle the question of Beatles or Stones, let's settle on some parameters. How about we break out the vaporizer and some of Colorado's greenest right now and then gauge each band on these fixed categories: Live Performance, Albums, Singles, Videos & Films, Looks & Style.

Go ahead, I'll wait.

I'll listen to some Zeppelin to cleanse the palate, so to speak. Something off, oh yeah, *Physical Graffiti*.

Ready?

Let's start the way both bands did, bringing it to us live in clubs and in concert, and on the radio and on TV.

The Stones have a sizable advantage in the live music category. While the Beatles were a terrific live band as their early recordings prove—check out their BBC sessions or any of the live bootlegs—they rocked while enduring abysmal sonic conditions of nonexistent or primitive sound systems. But they stopped gigging before reaching the height of their creativity. The Stones, on the other hand, have continually loved us live. Hell, the Stones' sound live on their studio albums, and those signature raw and stabbing counterpoint riffs, the fragmented chords, the shouted vocals, the interlocking grooves that sound so great on albums, often get bigger, looser, more outrageous and, yes, better when they are on stage. Meanwhile, they also delivered epic spectacles—with inflatable stage props that were outrageous in their size and their subject matter. With Jagger riding and humping a giant inflatable penis, or the gigantic inflatable golden naked woman in chains on the *Bridges to Babylon* tour, these creations became part of the definition of the Stones. Even now, 50 years on, this band of septuagenarians delivers raucous concerts in which Jagger, in particular, performs like a finger-wagging Olympian. Watching him roam the stage, it is not a stretch to wonder where he stands among the world's best senior citizen athletes.

So as great—and they were truly great—as the Beatles were live, it says here that the Stones have it all over the Beatles as a live band. And yes, I know the Beatles killed the Stones when it comes to live vocals. But this ain't *Glee,* and we are not running a choral competition.

As for rating the albums, again, this is an easy one. Easy, easy, easy. The Beatles released 12 studio albums while they were together over an eight-year span. And while I think *The Beatles* (a.k.a. The White Album) and *Let It Be* have a number of weak tracks, they also have some killer tracks. But by and large, Beatles albums are the greatest use of petroleum byproduct in the history of mankind. From those joyful, rockin' pop tunes on the early albums to the studio magic that fuels *Sgt. Pepper's Lonely Hearts Club Band*, there is so much to love about the Beatles' albums: groundbreaking instrumentation, ornate arrangements, and lyrics that have become literature. Seriously, have the Stones done anything on vinyl that matches the stunning cut-and-paste suite that dominates the second half of *Abbey Road*? With *Beggars Banquet, Let It Bleed, Sticky Fingers, Exile on Main Street, Some Girls, Tattoo You*—the Stones have made awesome albums over 50-plus years. But the output, the consistency, innovation, popular appeal and cultural and historical importance just isn't there to compete with *A Hard Day's Night, Help!, Rubber Soul, Revolver, Sgt. Pepper's Lonely Hearts Club Band, Magical Mystery Tour,* and *Abbey Road.* Stones defenders can rightfully note that the Beatles broke up before the release of *Saturday Night Fever* and therefore never felt the pressure to go through a disco phase. Too bad. Phases are part of the game. (I actually like the Stones' "Emotional Rescue" and "Undercover of the Night," but the albums they lend their names to aren't that great.) The Beatles, for instance, kicked the Stones' butt when it came to psychedelia.

Are you with me here? The score is Beatles 1, Stones 1.

So now let's look at their visual and stylistic sides.

Before you hear a band's music, you often see the band— or their album—first, via a photograph, record cover or, more recently, a video or gif. And both these bands have strong identities in the looks department. As a young kid, I had trouble telling the Beatles apart from one another. My kids had the same problem despite in-depth coaching from their crazy old man. In the early days, the boy band from Liverpool aimed for a uniform look. The Beatles had Beatle cuts, Beatle boots and tailored, matching outfits. They looked alike, and to a non-Liverpudlian, they sounded alike in interviews. While the Beatles eventually shed their Brian Epstein-masterminded uniform and mutated into various hippie incarnations, the Stones, who also were equally tough to distinguish in the early days, honed their look and hair into what now stands as *the* archetypal rock look. It is not surprising that Mick Jagger and Keith Richards call themselves the Glimmer *Twins.* For most of their careers, they have had matching physiques, black bangs and attitudes. And when craggy-faced, black-haired Ronnie Wood joined the band, you could be forgiven for wondering if this was a family act.

Fashion-wise, Mick and Keith have provided a style template to legions of hard rockers (including Steven Tyler and Axl Rose, to name two of the most prominent and derivative). But the Stones' visual identity also includes an enduring logo—lascivious "Tongue and Lips" drawing by British designer John Pasche. The Beatles can claim no such comparable crest—aside, maybe, from the capital drop-T in their name—but they do have *Sgt. Pepper* and *Abbey Road*, probably the most iconic album covers in music history.

So who wins this one? I have to call it a tie. The Stones have had the more consistent visual identity, no question. But the Beatles had equal, if not greater, visual power and influence in their day.

As far as singles go, the Beatles have scored more than double the amount of number 1's on the Billboard Hot 100 than the Stones. But should we hand the Fab Four a victory in this category based on sales and radio play? Is that any proof that one band is a "better" singles band than another? By that logic, Rihanna and Elvis Presley are better than the Beatles, as they have more number one hits. Also consider this: If a band releases a single and no one buys it or plays it on the radio, is it still a single? Yes, it is. And it could be the "best" single ever in the history of music. So chart rankings, although an attribute of a single, shall not be the sole determinant in this discussion.

What is a single, anyway? Singles came into being with the age of the long-playing album in the late 1940s. The 45 RPM single—a disc that could "fit" only one song on each side—arrived a year after the LP, which allowed for about 20 minutes of music on a side. Over time, a single became known as a song that is released by a band or record label with the idea that this song should receive special attention. (The record companies now give it even more attention by creating videos for the song, but let's not deal with that here—I only mention it because the video has become a major factor in boosting a single's popularity.) If a single is released off an album, it's usually because someone has decided that this particular song has a better chance of reaching and moving an audience than any of the other songs on the album. Therefore, it will have a better chance of garnering more radio play and selling more copies.

Since singles consist of music and lyrics and we are talking about who is the better singles band, we need to talk about the music and lyrics that make up those singles.

Before I first started pondering the lyrics question, I assumed John Lennon and Paul McCartney would trounce Mick and Keith. Bob Dylan elevated the rock song lyric to an art form and the Beatles were listening. In the hands of McCartney, lyrics are at times poetic and empathetic ("She's Leaving Home," "Eleanor Rigby") or sophisticated and witty ("When I'm Sixty-Four," "Lovely Rita") in a way that recall the best literate British music hall or Broadway show tunes. Meanwhile, Lennon's psychedelic verbal wizardry is spectacular. From "Tomorrow Never Knows" ("Turn off your mind, relax and float downstream") to "Lucy in the Sky with Diamonds" to "Being for the Benefit of Mr. Kite" to "I Am the Walrus," he is an entertaining, often humorous, trippy surrealist. Even their backup songwriter, George Harrison, delivered one of their finest love songs with "Something," and one of their edgiest with "Taxman" ("If you take a walk, I'll tax your feet.")

But look at the lyrics of the Glimmer Twins, and you'll find plenty of ass-kicking songwriting.

Humor is where the bad-boy Stones actually give the fun-loving Beatles a run for the money. "I went down to the demonstration/to get my fair share of abuse," deadpans Jagger in "You Can't Always Get What You Want." It's a brilliant line that can cut a number of ways. Decades later, it still reverberates even if you're not part of Occupy Wall Street or a disillusioned Arab Spring protester. While Lennon has been cited for his caustic eye, Jagger's frustrated observations in "Satisfaction" ("and a man comes on and tells me how white my shirts can be/but he can't be a man 'cause he doesn't smoke the same cigarettes as me") have a cynical black humor that rings true 50 years later. The chorus of "Get Off of My Cloud," in which he dismisses everyone by saying "two's a crowd," broaches the mathematical wit of "Eight Days a Week." And Jagger's cornpone American-accented send-up in the intro of "Far Away Eyes" hits a comedy high Paul McCartney only dreamed of when he wrote "Rocky Raccoon."

Equally inventive but much more serious in intent and scope, "Sympathy for the Devil" delivers a stunning lyric from Jagger, who has variously said he was trying to channel Dylan and that the song was influenced by Baudelaire. He's also given a nod to Russian author Mikhail Bulgakov's novel *The Master and Margarita*, which tells the story of the Devil's visit to the Soviet Union. Jagger says he was trying to adopt the persona of Lucifer and he sounds sinister and possessed, delivering a sprawling overview of history's hellish moments from the death of Christ to World War II. When he indicts his listeners—"I shouted out, 'Who killed the Kennedys?'/When after all, it was you and me"—it is arguably as biting as anything the Beatles ever wrote.

Which makes the lyrics aspect of this debate a lot closer than anyone might have thought. Ultimately the consistency, variety and output over a mere eight years earns the Beatles the right to claim they are the better lyricists, but just barely. From "Under My Thumb," to "Street Fighting Man" to "Some Girls" to "Shattered," Jagger and Richards are gritty rock neorealists compared to their more arty rivals.

So onto the second part of the singles equation: the music. The success of a single can be based on a number of things: hype, lyrics, videos, airplay and, finally, music: the melody, the beat, the chorus and the hook, which is usually a music phrase (riff) or melody that catches the ear. A hook can be part of the chorus. It can be the intro. It can appear anywhere and it is what truly makes a single a single.

When it comes to catching the ear, the Stones—and Keith Richards in particular—are kings of the riff. The fuzzed out guitar figure in "Satisfaction" that propelled the Stones to their first number one hit was just the beginning. "Can't You Hear Me Knocking," "Jumpin' Jack Flash," and "Start Me Up" all feature indelible riffs that are rough, bruising, textured, rhythmically gripping signature sounds. The Beatles have some great hooks, too—"Day Tripper," "Tomorrow Never Knows"—but most of their hooks are tied to vocals and melody. On "Hey Jude," the outro-chorus of "Na, Na-na, na-na-na-na" may in fact be the most sticky hook ever written. I like to think of it as the Lord's Prayer of rock—it's impossible not to join in when you hear it. And the opening of every verse is pretty hooky and hard to miss, too: "Hey Jude."

As brilliant as "Hey Jude" is, it doesn't "rock" like the Rolling Stones' hooks rock. The major-to-suspended chords that open "Start Me Up" or send "Gimme Shelter" into overdrive are a case in point. They carry stylistic DNA that is instantly memorable and identifiable as a Stones sound. Countless bands use the same chords, but the sonic grit and grime on the slashing, rhythmic hooks is just, well, *Stonesian*. Similarly, the opening of "Honky Tonk Women," a syncopated duet of cowbell and trap drums, creates an impossibly funky groove that the rest of the band can slam into. It's primal.

That hook ability leads me to say, yet again, it's a close call. But while I gave the Mop Tops the lyrical trophy when it comes to singles, the music side of this unofficial Olympic event has to go to the Stones. Their riffs are better than the other guys'.

Again, I'm sure there are a lot people shaking their head and thinking about, say, the glory that is "Day Tripper." The Beatles' music is tremendous. It is. Even if George Martin scored some of it for them, it is amazing. But we are talking singles here. Not album tracks.

And that means that singles ends up a tie.

So we are even-Steven going into the last category: Video. Or let's call it film and video.

The lads from Liverpool made the most influential rock movie ever with *A Hard Day's Night*. Its jump cuts, hand-held cameras, rhythmic editing, and—for the time—anarchic feel make it a landmark film. This was not the first jukebox movie— Elvis started releasing them in the late '50s. But *A Hard Day's Night* was the freshest music flick of its time, and it inspired *The Monkees* TV series, not to mention the follow-up Beatles film, *Help*.

And as noted, the Beatles also made arguably the first rock videos with their promo *Magical Mystery Tour*, featuring hazy, often non-narrative footage and avant-garde, psychedelic visuals.

The Stones, not to be outdone on the avant-garde cinema front, worked with Jean-Luc Godard on his film *One Plus*

*One*—later retitled *Sympathy for the Devil*—featuring footage of the band recording the title song, footage of Black Panthers, and curious interviews on the soundtrack with a woman named Eve Democracy. It's a more overtly political work of art—thanks, no doubt, to Godard—than pretty much anything the Beatles ever engaged in, with the possible exception of John Lennon and Yoko Ono's Bed-In.

The Stones, clearly fans of the auteur theory, then worked with Maysles brothers on one of the most famous and influential rock documentaries in history, *Gimme Shelter*. The movie captures the ugliness of rock excess with footage of a horrifying murder in the crowd during a Stones show. They also hired Martin Scorsese—who uses the title track in three of his movies, *Goodfellas, Casino* and *The Departed*—to direct their 2010 concert film, *Shine a Light*—which, ironically, doesn't feature his favorite Stones tune.

The Beatles' final cinematic move was to make *Let It Be*. But ultimately, the band decided not to let *Let It Be* actually be. The film, widely and correctly viewed as disappointing—although many find it a fascinating record of the band's building resentment toward Paul—hasn't been available for the home video market since the 1980s. Meanwhile, the Stones film *Cocksucker Blues* caught the bad boys being so bad, they went to court to stop it from being screened.

As for video, the Stones made "Waiting on a Friend," a notably low-key video in the early MTV age, that opens with a shot of Mick Jagger standing in a doorway on a vaguely familiar-looking stoop in New York's East Village—one of the two stoops that appear on the cover of Led Zeppelin's legendary album, ahem, *Physical Graffiti*. This easygoing clip shows Keith arriving, embracing Mick and shaking hands with reggae great Peter Tosh, who is sitting on the stoop. Then the two Stones amble down the street. The video winds up celebrating the camaraderie of a band, as the Stones meet up, hang out, and jam at the St. Marks Bar & Grill, a place where I used to drink a lot back in the days when I used to drink a lot.

Uh-oh, did I just inject a totally arbitrary and personal fact in that last comment? I did!

And I did that on purpose because, well, we can *try* to be rational and objective about bands and their music. And even if we succeed in that impossible task, there's another fact clouding the Beatles or Stones decision: the fact that just as we define bands, *we also use bands to define ourselves.*

Not to get too eggheaded about it, but self-definition, or personal identity, consists of determining the properties that make us who we are. Personal identity is to some extent a fluid construct—you can change. These days you can change your name, your gender, and, if you are a person of questionable intelligence who hates guitars, you can even go from listening to rock to listening to techno or dubstep, whatever that is. And bands like the Beatles and the Stones change, too. But their work, their look, their albums, their gigs are fixed in time and space. And we use those fixed properties as the points of reference when we are faced with that ultimate question: Beatles or Stones?

We make associations with the properties of these bands and latch on to them. Am I proud to have been in the dive bar where the Stones shot a video to a great song that also features a lovely sax solo from jazz great Sonny Rollins? Well, let's say I'm glad I can make that association, and that I know some of the fragments of that particular part of the Stones puzzle. It gives me yet another bond with the song, the video and *Tattoo*

*You*—the album on which "Waiting on a Friend" appears—and of course the band that made it. But even it if wasn't shot in the St. Marks Bar & Grill, it would still be a favorite, because I have judged and admired other properties of the song: the laid-back, country-meets-bossa nova groove, the roadhouse keyboards, the lyrics about connections, and the casual, low-key chorus. To me, it is a perfectly balanced song with music underscoring the lyrics and vice versa.

Everyone has connections to bands and music in this way. Recognizing a song after hearing just the first measure is an act of self-definition. You know the song! You are knowledgeable. It is an aspect of you. And if you like the song, or hate it—and we will discuss how those preferences are shaped in a chapter about Rush—that is an aspect of you, too, of your taste and critical thinking. Or maybe your lack of taste and your lack of critical thinking.

Your feelings about all things Beatles and all things Stones are properties of you, not properties of those respective bands. True, the bands and the music inspired those feelings. But those feelings also could have been inspired by the cool dude on the school bus with the Tongue and Lips logo on his backpack, or your cousin who could strum along to every John and Paul song in the catalog, or the memory of three girls joyfully singing and splashing "She loves you, yeah, yeah, yeah" while playing in the town swimming pool.

I haven't talked about which band looks better, cuter, or sexier. I haven't talked about rebelliousness and the different modes of rebellion. George Harrison's embrace of Eastern religion flew in the face of established cultural norms, and so did Keith Richard's drug use. And so if you gravitate toward the spiritual, maybe Beatles is your answer because you attach importance to that attribute. Or maybe you love a bad boy, so Stones is your answer.

Or maybe you suffer from the affliction of being a drummer—and we will delve deeper into the sad, humiliating existential reality of being a drummer, don't worry—and to you, this question immediately translates into the question of Ringo Starr or Charlie Watts? Of course, that answer—as any drummer aware that the primary function of a drummer is to keep time and serve the song knows—is: both. They are both utterly awesome.

I, too, feel torn by this Big Question. I love both bands. I love Ringo and Charlie. I love Mick and Paul and Keith and John. At times, struggling with Beatles or Stones, I mutate the question. I ask myself which band I'd rather be in. And every single time, I decide if I could be in the Stones while they toured but record with the Beatles, that would be the perfect solution. But the question—Beatles or Stones?—doesn't give me that out.

You've probably noticed that my attempted impartial accounting of Beatles or Stones has basically ended in a draw. I tried to be objective, to stay with something akin to the facts, and came up with a tie. But there can't be a tie. That wouldn't answer the question. "Both" is not part of the question, so it's not an option.

I DO HAVE AN ANSWER, EVEN IF IT DISAPPOINTS ME A LITTLE, because as empirical and objective as I want to be, the answer is shaped not just by my judicious, critical analysis; there are external forces at work here. There are attributes—like context, repetition and environment—that influence the answer. Familiarity is a huge factor in liking and appreciating music. Studies have shown that the more you hear a song, the greater the chance you will like it. Most listeners prefer to hear music they know as opposed to new music. Someone raised in Nashville on twangy country music is unlikely to immediately embrace the stratospherically shrill singing in Bollywood songs of the 1970s. The more you hear it, the more entrenched and embraceable a sound becomes.

In the micromanaged world of contemporary radio, the Stones and the Beatles are both classified as Classic Rock bands. A 2014 survey of classic rock radio by the data-crunching website fivethirtyeight.com determined that songs by the Rolling Stones represented 3 percent of the music played on classic rock radio across the country, a number that ranked them behind Aerosmith and Van Halen (neither of whom is the answer to Beatles or Stones, by the way; although each of those bands owe a great deal to the Rolling Stones for their circus-like live shows). The Beatles? They finished 9th with 1.9 percent of the airplay.

I raise this point not as evidence of the Stones reigning supreme over the Beatles, but to show just how much airplay they get. Five out of every 100 songs—or one out of every 20 songs—on classic rock radio are Stones or Beatles. Considering they represent a minuscule section of available recorded music, this is some serious cultural bombardment. If you listen to Classic Rock radio, there's a good chance that every two hours you are going to hear a song by the Beatles or the Stones.

• • •

YOU KNOW THE ANSWER TO BEATLES OR STONES BECAUSE IT rests with you. This is not a cop-out. Radio play currently says the Stones. Records sales, historically, say the Beatles. The question is personal and the answer can only be personal.

Because of my associations with the don't-give-a-damn coolness of their rebellious sound and image, my head leans Stones. They are just way more hypnotic, sexier and more dangerous than the Beatles. When I look at the songs, the singing, the music, the looks, the humor, the genius, the overriding joy and poignancy of the music and, yes, the love that permeates through so much of their work, my heart beats—involuntarily —for the Beatles. They are part of me. Perhaps I can blame the imprinting of *Revolver* and *Sgt. Pepper* on my 8-year-old-brain as I studied my parents' album covers and absorbed the music over and over (the only Stones album they had while I was growing up was the bluesy *Out of Our Heads*). But the properties of the Beatles, for me, win out. Taken in total, their attributes speak to me louder and more clearly than the attributes of the Stones do. In my heart's eye, I'm not a bad boy and I'm not a mop top either. I'm an arty guy. I like to read, I'd be too scared to do hard drugs, and (tragically) girls are not going to gravitate toward me because I seem like a sexy and dangerous guy who knows the pleasures of evil. I'm not. I don't. Sniff. So the fact is, the Beatles reflect my interest in music and culture more than the Stones do. They are more a part of me than the other guys.

So: Beatles.

Your experience may differ.

# WHAT KIND OF AIR GUITAR DO YOU PLAY? OR THE QUESTION OF REALITY

IF YOU ARE LIKE ME AND HAVE NEVER ACTUALLY STUDIED philosophy, but you have friends who have, you probably know that sometimes philosophers tell stories to make a point, or to provide a fresh perspective, or to inspire students to draw their own conclusions. And sometimes a story is welcome to just change things up because philosophy can make your head spin. So, here is a story. I guess you could call it a fable. Or maybe I mean a parable. Or let's just call it a launching point for ... something. Anyway, read the story, and then we'll dig into air guitars, one of the greatest musical inventions of the late 20th century.

# MORE THAN A FEELING

*The new Air Guitar Center at the mall has a fifty-foot wall lined with 200 air guitars, each with a placard identifying the name, model and year of each artificial axe. There are two air guitar techs—one named Buzz and the other named Wire—who are on hand to discuss anything and everything related to the riff machines.*

*The Air Guitar Center has a stage surrounded by mirrors on three sides. The back mirror is just a normal mirror. But the "rocking glasses," as Buzz calls them, on both sides of the stage are funhouse mirrors.*

*Stage left is a fat mirror. Stage right is a skinny mirror. At some angles you can see your skinny self with your air guitar reflecting across the stage into the fat mirror and then back again into the skinny mirror, and so on and so forth.*

*"It's kind of like the visual equivalent of a delay pedal that is set to infinite repeat as you play a minor chord then a major chord," says Wire.*

*"That is a beautiful thing," says Buzz, with a blissed-out look in his eyes. "Going minor to major."*

*It costs $8 to play a song on the stage, with the air guitar of your choice.*

*A kid comes into The Air Guitar Center and asks to try the 1967 Flying V air guitar with the cherry red finish. Buzz slides a ladder over and carefully brings down the air Flying V.*

*"This is really nice," the kid says, pulling the air strap over his head.*

*"It's more than nice," says Buzz. "It's like the third best feeling in the world."*

*"What are the other two?" asks the kid.*

*"Number one is sex with someone you love. Sex in general is number two. And sometimes it's actually reversed, so that sex with someone you don't love can be number one."*

*The kid rolls his eyes.*

*"It's complicated," Buzz adds.*

*"Buzz, man, the dude is, like, 12 years old," says Wire.*

*"He asked. Look, dude, go try it out."*

*The kid goes onto the stage and Wire hits some switches on the mixing and light boards.*

*"What do you want to play, dude?" Wire asks.*

*" 'Back in Black,' " says the kid.*

*"We heard that four times today. Choose another."*

*"Aw, come on. I paid my eight bucks!"*

*"Read The Air Guitar Center rules, dude. 'In accordance with Geneva Convention rules against torture, no song shall be played more than 4 times in a day.'"*

*" 'More Than a Feeling.' "*

*"Jesus Christ," says Buzz.*

*"Okay," sighs Wire. "We've only heard that twice today."*

*The kid starts out rough. The younger ones always do. They don't have the chops, the smoothness, the hours of mirror time you need to be a great air guitarist. Wire cuts the music in the middle of the greatest acoustic intro north of "Stairway."*

*"What?" says the kid.*

*"You're playing it too high, dude. Adjust the strap. The air Flying V looks stupid up high. Unless you want to look like the nerdy guitarist in Cheap Trick. Do you want that?"*

*The kid shakes his head and lowers his hands.*

*"And remember, don't freak out during the intro. It's sensitive."*

The kid gets it. He's air finger picking, which is much cooler than using an air pick for this part of the song. He's swaying his head, which is the appropriate melodic move, as opposed to bopping his head up and down, which usually works better with a chorus. Then he stops air playing right before the Boston singer closes his eyes and slips away.

"What?" asks Wire.

"I should be playing a double-neck, so I can switch between an acoustic and a six-string."

"You have a point," says Buzz. "But these days, we can just process your signal with FX on the board, dude. Wire will handle it with a harmonizer on the mixing board."

"But—"

"Look, kid, we had the air guitar you are talking about. But yesterday this older guy wanted it for 'Pinball Wizard.' He went all early Pete Townshend on us and smashed it to bits. We had to call the cops."

"Come on," Wire says, cuing the Boston song. "There are other people waiting."

The kid air finger picks and sways, then knee slides across the stage while hitting the song's epic pre-chorus lead. Dowh, dowh, dowh-dowh-dowh. Dowh-dowh-dowhdowhdowh DOWH!! Then he's on his feet, bouncing up and down and mouthing the backing vocals on the chorus until it's time for the first solo, which he plays with the air Flying V behind his head while doing fast-twitch hip-hop footwork.

"Nice!" says Buzz. "Air dancing!"

After the Boston singer is "tired and thinking cold," whatever that is, and dreaming about a girl he used to know but who slips away when he closes his eyes, the kid walks across the stage, strafing *the imaginary audience with the notes off his air Flying V. Then he mouths the outro chorus and Wire even cranks the smoke machine and strobes for him at the end.*

*When he's done, the kid says, "I think that's probably the fourth best feeling."*

*"How's that?" asks Buzz.*

*"You forgot eating ice cream on a hot day," he says, handing back the air Flying V.*

*Buzz takes it. Wire waits for his pal to lecture the kid, but instead Buzz says. "You are right. I stand corrected. That's more than a feeling, too, right?"*

*The kid nods earnestly. He might even be 11.*

*"Exactly," he says.*

IF THIS WERE A LITERATURE CLASS, I WOULD ASK YOU TO WRITE an essay explaining what the point of this story was. But since you paid money for this book—unless you got this book as a gift, took it out of the library or stole it—I'll just tell you.

Originally, the point of the story was to explore what I thought was a funny idea—the Air Guitar Center—so I wrote it. I didn't actually think about why it was funny. It just was. But as I wrote the piece, it began to take on more meaning for me. I started thinking about the sometimes heroic and sometimes moronic guys who toil in music stores, listening to repetitive riffs over and over. I thought about the song "More Than a Feeling," and why it is not only such a great air guitar song because playing air guitar is very much about feeling music. But it is a profound lyric, too. What is more than a feeling? Is a feeling a hunch or something with an edge of doubt? Or is more than a feeling a certainty? Is it reality? Or did Tom Scholz, the songwriter in Boston, mean it was "better" than a feeling? I thought about sex, because I often think about sex, and sex is also about feeling. I thought about air guitar itself—the joyous physical interpretation and embodiment of a song through that constantly maligned art form, mime. And then I thought, wow, playing air guitar is both playing an instrument and playing (as in having fun) and yet not actually, physically, playing at all. And I realized I had blown my own mind and might blow yours, too.

That's because, to probably put too fine a point on it, air guitar challenges our notions of reality. The act of playing air guitar does something more complex than make the person playing air guitar look like a fool and an idiot. On one level it allows a physical response to music for fans of a given song, riff or solo. But on another level, air guitar makes fantasy reality, it takes an imaginary construct that is based on a real construct—playing an actual guitar—and makes it a concrete action; in other words, something that is fake becomes real while also remaining fake. In this way air guitar threatens to confound reality.

What the fuck am I talking about? Let's back up.

Way up.

All the way to Plato.

Plato is older and possibly wiser than Louis Jordan, one of the genius elders of rock 'n' roll. He is even older than jazz and classical music put together. A student of the Greek philosopher Socrates, Plato was one of the first men known to try to define reality. His plan of attack was to discuss what exists in the world and how we define what exists in the world. To be totally honest, Platonic realism is somewhat confusing at the outset because you have to learn new terminology, starting with particulars. A guitar, a car, a cat, a copy of *Dark Side of the Moon,* or a ticket to see the 54th reunion tour of the Who—these are all particulars. For now, think of particulars as objects. Objects have properties that define them: shape, color, design, materials. Or perhaps I should say, *help* define them; different guitars have different properties— some have square-shaped bodies, some have rounded bodies. Some guitars have 12 strings, most have six, and Keith Richards sometimes plays with five. So a particular is the sum of various properties, and not just the sum, but often a unified aggregation of properties in a fixed or consistent manner or shape. All electric guitars have bodies, necks, headstocks, and strings. And while those different components may have different colors or shapes, they are assembled in generally the same structure—body, neck, headstock—which we all recognize as a guitar.

Let's take a dog—a beagle, say—as our particular and strip it of its properties: no fur, no tail, no short legs, no long body, or no floppy ears or lovable, down-on-its-luck expression. Without those properties, it's nothing. There is no dog, no beagle. But put those properties together and you've got yourself a new best friend. Actually, you don't even need to put those properties together in a physical sense, because we still have the ability to envision a beagle. The properties of beagle—proportionality, the shape and floppiness of the ears, the fur—can be imagined. Plato called these properties universals.

Now let's conjure up a guitar. Let's take that Flying V from 1967 with a cherry finish. A truly marvelous, wonderfully absurd object. If you take away the strings, the neck, the headstock and machine heads, the whammy bar, and the V-shaped body with the knobs and the pickups, what have you got?

Nothing, right?
Wait a minute, that's not nothing.
That's an air guitar!

THE AIR GUITAR PLAYS WITH ASSUMPTIONS OF REALITY IN A number of ways. It is an abstraction of a real thing, a guitar. "More Than a Feeling," the story you just read, is funny in part because the story assumes that a total abstraction that cannot, by definition, exist in a physical state—if air guitars had actual mass and were tactile, they would not be air guitars—is generally treated like a real, physical thing.[1]

How can something that doesn't exist be real?

The story riffs, if you'll pardon the expression, on this idea without ever confronting it. It accepts the air guitar as a real thing. Interestingly, we all know that playing air guitar is real; we've seen people do it. Hell, you've probably done it. So, theoretically, preposterously, we can say that air guitars—the nonexistent thing that is being "played"—exist. But they can't exist, because the joke and joy of playing air guitar is that there's nothing there.

---

1   What is the Platonic ideal of the electric guitar? Like the Beatles or Stones, the perfect electric guitar is a personal choice based on aesthetics (does it look "cool"), idolatry (who else plays this type of guitar), sound, and feel. The world is broken into a number of camps: the Fender Stratocaster camp, the Fender Telecaster camp, the Gibson Les Paul camp, and the this-guitar-looks-fucking-cool camp (see Danelectro, Silvertone, steel guitars, Flying V). They are all fine camps to belong to. Even though I have a '72 Strat and an Ibanez semi-hollow body E-35, I sometimes pine for the Gibson SG of my youth. It's light. It's cheap. It has an even, balanced, sensual shape. And it is what Angus Young of AC/DC rocks with.

There are many things that are real but that don't have a physical presence. Ideas, theories, jokes, stories, history, philosophy. We can say, then, that air guitars can exist as an idea, and an idea is something that is real, that is willed into existence, an offshoot of French philosopher Rene Descartes' "I think, therefore I am." With air guitar, it's more like "I pretend to rock, therefore it is."

Of course, for most readers, air guitars probably didn't exist until I placed them in the story. Most people don't envision the kind of guitar they are playing when they mime to music. They just do it. That's another comical thing about the story. It takes a fantastical element and brings it into reality, or if not reality, something familiar (there is no Air Guitar Center, but there is a Guitar Center). The whole thing is absurd, right? But that was my goal: to amuse you with bizarre notions of an alternate musical reality and make you think about playing air guitar. And ask you: Really, what kind of air guitar do you play?

# BILLY JOEL, REALLY? OR THE QUESTION OF AUTHENTICITY

## A MORONIC DIALOGUE

*I'm driving with my 15-year-old son, flipping through the radio. We laugh about the 24-hour cliché network that is sports radio, lame acoustic guitar intros, Jamaican DJs who constantly interrupt the songs they are playing, and how much "Rock Me Gently" by Andy Kim sounds exactly like Neil Diamond, except for the lame funky electric piano break at the end of the song, which Neil would never have allowed.*

*And then "You May Be Right," by Billy Joel, comes on, and my son starts singing along.*

*I pull over to the side of the road.*

"Son," I say, turning the radio off, "I think it's time we have a real heart to heart."

"Oh no. Not about the birds and bees," my son laughs.

"No, we had that talk already."

"Did we?"

"Sort of. I talked to you about porn and sex."

"Oh yeah."

"You remember?"

"'Don't be a disrespectful jerk. Women want to be listened to and are God's gift to men. Porn is not to be looked at as an ABC primer for sex. Always wear a condom.'"

"Well done. You forgot one thing."

"I'm not supposed to be afraid to ask you anything."

"Excellent. You do listen."

He takes a deep breath. "So what is this talk going to be about?"

"About Billy Joel."

"What?"

"You can't go around singing Billy Joel in public. Or even in the car."

"Come on, Dad."

"I know it's not in any parenting books, but it's true. Just take it from me."

"Why do you hate Billy Joel?"

"Does everything have to have a reason?"

"When I say that, you always say yes."

"Some things are just true."

"So this isn't a talk. It's a lecture."

He's a smart kid, my son, except for this Billy Joel thing. I don't know where to start, so I say the first thing that comes into my head: "First of all, he has two first names."

*"So does Elton John."*

*"Elton John is a stage name. It's a joke. It's rock 'n' roll."*

*"That's a stupid reason. What else?"*

*"Too much piano. Not enough rock."*

*"Elton plays piano. Little Richard plays piano, Monk plays piano."*

*"But all those guys rock. Billy Joel has never really rocked. He has rollicked on 'Piano Man,' but he has never rocked, not even on 'Only the Good Die Young.' That is why you shouldn't sing him. It's emasculating. Just promise me: no singing Billy Joel."*

*"That's absurd. You sing stuff from* Sound of Music.*"*

*"So did Coltrane. But Julie Andrews rocks, too. She brings it. She owns it. She has more in common with Hendrix than Billy Joel does. I know it's hard to do that math, but it's true."*

*"You sing along to friggin' Karen Carpenter. How is that any better than Billy Joel? And he's better than the Beach Boys. Jeez, that's like listening to the Mormon Tabernacle Choir sometimes. It's so bland and funkless."* Then he makes a mock professorial voice: *"'*Pet Sounds *is the apotheosis of pop.' Give me a break."*

*I remind myself that he's 15 and that I was a musical nimrod at 15. I thought a cassette tape of* Infinity *by Journey was a good thing, not realizing it was a sonic war crime until I was, like, 16.*

*"Son, maybe when you are older, you'll understand. It's hard to quantify. But taking pot shots at Brian Wilson is not going to score points with anyone who knows anything about music."*

*"Billy Joel is a smart pop songwriter. I think you are wrong."*

*"He is a talented showman, a craftsman. No question. But that's the problem. There's no there there. Karen Carpenter was singing her life, man."*

*"What? With 'I'm on the Top of the World?'"* he snorts.

*"Listen to 'Superstar.' You'll hear it."*

*"Can we drive? I'm going to sing whatever I want. I can't believe you are a Billy Joelcist!"*

*I put the car in drive and we head home in silence.*

*I don't want to alienate my son over music. That's one thing we share. And it's absurd to expect that one generation will think like the next when it comes to pop music. I open my yap with a peace offering:*

*"You may be right," I say.*

*"No question."*

*"I may be crazy."*

*He doesn't say anything. Doesn't crack a smile. Doesn't even look at me for quoting the lyrics of a Billy Joel hit. He looks out the window.*

*I park and we get out of the car and walk toward home.*

*"Dad?" he says.*

*"Yes?"*

*"Was that a concession speech?"*

It was not a concession speech.

The question of Billy Joel is, like Beatles or Stones, a dividing line. Few pop stars have been as divisive a figure as Billy Joel. Many critics detest him, which is interesting because writing about Joel poses a unique challenge: It is extremely difficult to write about the meaning of Billy Joel in rock because it requires listening to Billy Joel, which historically speaking, very few rock writers have wanted to do.

And that reluctance is not because Mr. Joel once tore up a review written by *New York Times* critic Robert Palmer in front of 20,000-odd people at Madison Square Garden. Really, many rock writers would probably claim that as a badge of honor.

No, the reluctance comes with having to address the schism of Pop Pastiche versus the Real Thing. For many, Billy Joel's relationship to rock is similar to that of margarine to butter. Or, let us defer to that aforementioned ripped-up review, a critique of a 1980 Joel concert, in which Palmer wrote: "Rock and Roll and Mr. Joel have about as much in common as a Beethoven Symphony and a sneeze."

No wonder "Mr. Joel" shredded the review.

But Palmer hasn't been the only hater.

In 1970 Billy Joel released his first album, a rock record under the noxious band name Attila. This was a keyboard-driven metal duo, with Joel doing triple duty: He sang, played his electrified ivories, and even laid down keyboard bass lines. The record is now a punch line. Critic Stephen Thomas Erlewine, writing for the *All Music Guide*, put it this way: "*Attila* undoubtedly is the worst album released in the history of rock 'n' roll—hell, the history of recorded music itself. There have been many bad ideas in rock, but none match the colossal stupidity of *Attila*." Erlewine wrote his review in hindsight, long after Billy Joel became a Top 40 star. But it's hard to argue with his take on the record. It is horrible. Joel himself has referred to the album as "psychedelic bullshit," although to be fair, he really shouldn't tar psychedelia with the same brush as Attila.

Tom Moon, author of *1,000 Recordings to Hear Before You Die*, failed to include a single Billy Joel recording in his book. "I actually went and listened to *The Stranger* and *52nd Street* and *Glass Houses* and a couple of Billy Joel records in pieces," said Moon, explaining the omission to an interviewer, "and came to the conclusion: 'You know what? These records are flawed.' And as great as some of the songwriting is, as a full album experience I couldn't find it."

The list of assaults on Joel is long. Ron Rosenbaum's article "The Worst Pop Singer Ever" exposes the underlying contempt that lies beneath Joel lyrics. Robert Christgau once called him "pure Tin Pan Alley," but later opined that Joel is "a force of nature and bad taste."

As Moon indicates, Joel is a talented man. He can write songs. Some of them are clever. Some are funny. Some are sentimental, and some are really, really awful. Many of them have become huge hits. But any idea that he is a rocker is diminished by the wide variety of his music—the troubadour brio of "Piano Man," the slick doo-wop-lite of "Uptown Girl," the corrosive sweetness of "She's Always a Woman," the modestly upbeat "Only the Good Die Young"—and the fact that so much of the work sounds ready for Broadway. All of this feeds into a decidedly unrocker image that comes with writing light, white and Top 40-friendly music.

The problem with Billy Joel, you see, is that the artist and his body of work raise questions of authenticity.

What is authenticity? The standard definition sees the term as synonymous with originality. But origin is not the issue here. The songs of Billy Joel are written by Billy Joel. He created, or originated, them. They are, in that sense of the word, authentic Billy Joel songs. But "authentic" has evolved in cultural and philosophical circles to touch on something more existential: It now connotes an emotionally appropriate, purposeful, natural extension of life and origin. The opposite of authentic is faux or false or fake or inorganic. Insincere.

Often when we say something rings false, we are not saying it is "wrong" or "incorrect." We are raising a flag about authenticity and sincerity. The false thing is an element or aspect that is not natural. Billy Joel's identity as a Top 40 schmaltzmeister makes it difficult, if not impossible, for rockers and critics to listen to his varied songs as anything other than Top 40 schmaltz.

Joel himself has lent fuel to the fire that engulfs him. "I know I've been referred to as derivative. Well, I'm damn guilty. I'm derivative as hell."

Plenty of other vaunted musicians and stars are sound-shifters. Paul McCartney writes oratorios and silly love songs and still burns up "Helter Skelter" and nobody accuses any of his creative choices as being inauthentic. It's just Paul being the same old experimental Beatle. When Paul Simon embarks on *Graceland* or *The Capeman*, or records with goddamned panpipes, the perception is it's all of a piece. There goes rhymin' Simon, appropriating other musical styles and recasting/interpreting them as his own. Of all the other popular, style-hopping stars, only Sting sets off alarms of inauthenticity and pretension. A great songwriter with the Police, his later work eschews the energy and sophisticated simplicity of the early years, replacing those hooks with more soulful, jazzy music that may be technically more complex but is infinitely more boring. (It may in fact be the Sting of today is the "real" Sting, while his turn as the peroxide blond leader of the Police was nothing more than a pre-fab punk-pop money-grab.)

The career and music of Elton John bears a number of stylistic and evolutionary similarities to Billy Joel. They both launched solo careers as sensitive singer-songwriter types before evolving into Top 40 production lines. But the two men's music and attitudes are completely different. After his album *Tumbleweed Connection*, John embraced the flamboyance, attitude and excess of glam rock in his music, his looks and his stagecraft. His best songs have a sizzle and majesty that Joel's lack. The lyrics are not his, but the vulnerable and soaring vocals on "Rocket Man" sure are; the in-your-face attitude on "The Bitch Is Back" sure is, and even though the idea of Lil' Elton rampaging is preposterous, he had the energy and edge to get "Saturday Night's Alright for Fighting" over without anyone choking from laughter.

Conversely, when Joel asks in a reverb-saturated voice meant to recall '50s recordings on "It's Still Rock and Roll to Me," "What's the matter with the clothes I'm wearing?" he sounds as combative as an insurance salesman trying to sell you a policy. Rock 'n' roll, ideally, has an edge, a backbeat you can use. All of that is sorely missing in the song. Joel's edgeless defense of rock 'n' roll makes it hard to place in rock's canon.

The onslaught of negative reviews in the major press impelled Joel to actually hire big shot publicist Howard Bloom and a Bloom protégée, former rock writer Elaine Shock, to sway the music intelligentsia. But if you have to arrange for a publicity campaign to adjust the public's perception of you, how authentic are you? The existence of the campaign to prove authenticity is intrinsically inauthentic. It could be argued, however, that the heart of rock 'n' roll is the hype—an idea we'll explore in a later chapter—and in an age of contrived and often mutating personas, a cynic might say nothing is more authentically rock 'n' roll than PR hype. But as all rockheads know, this is very wrong. Jimi Hendrix might have been a showman. And Jimi's manager might have been a Svengali, but his sound was unquestionably original. Ditto for Malcolm

McLaren and the Sex Pistols. The same could be said of the Beatles, who were the world's greatest boy band before they became the world's greatest songwriters and rock stars. They had a hypemeister in manager Brian Epstein. But they matched the hype and then some.

Billy Joel, really? Is he Attila? Or the Piano Man, or an angry rock purist throwing stones at glass houses? Or a sappy, earnest balladeer? Or is he the guy who wrote the 11-minute-plus prog-rock sounding "Hour of the Wolf" as a teenager with a band called the Hassles? It turns out Billy Joel never finished high school. This music-or-bust, anti-establishment credential is the kind of thing that should help establish rock authenticity. Then there was that Attila record—an unabashed rock move. But it has done Joel no good.

He also married a supermodel, which is, in fact, another authentic rock star rite—but even his ode to Christie Brinkley, "Uptown Girl," feels false. Why? Because the stance of the song and the phrase "Uptown Girl," implies that the singer is not an Uptown Boy. Therefore the listener likely assumes the singer is a downtown boy. Downtown, in this case, being a hipper opposite of the alleged bewitching, self-absorbed elegance of the Uptown Girl. But there's a problem for this semi-autobiographical song: The singer and writer is, in fact, a bridge-and-tunnel suburban Long Island boy.

All of this might suggest he is in no position to point fingers about geographically adduced stereotypes. But he does so anyway, because, hey, it's a song. It comes from a real place—Billy Joel's heart and head.

And that is the ultimate conundrum. Billy Joel may not appear to music cognoscenti as an authentic rocker, Attila aside, because he has become a craftsman.

An *authentic* craftsman.

The rock critics of the world don't owe Billy Joel an apology. But sometimes, in moments of weakness and compassion, I think we should be able to muster a grudging nod of respect to a craftsman, right? His work, like that of tunesmiths everywhere, comes out of sense and sensibility. His songs are real songs, with hooks, choruses, points of view and catch phrases. They are *seemingly* well-constructed songs. And some of them are rock songs, albeit with a meek backbeat, and barely audible electric guitars.

So let's go back to the question of Beatles or Stones, and the idea that how we feel about music is not just about the music. It is about projected and received images, about identity, about sincerity, about repetition and familiarity. All those things add to the context in which a song is played and heard. The singer brings his or her history, and you bring your history, plus your history with the singer's history.

These things are not easy to separate. Still, when I try to decontextualize the work of Billy Joel, I have flashes of doubt. The melodies, I have to concede, are generally strong. "Piano Man," despite rampant clichés (imagine Steely Dan writing the same song; it would be far more sinister and entertaining), is a fine rollicking barroom waltz. "Big Shot" recalls the stabbing rhythmic chording of evocative Elton John. Joel's McCartney-like ballads are fairly competent, although "She's Always a Woman"—which also owes a slight nod to Dylan's acidic "Just Like a Woman"—is a cringe-fest of sentimentality.

You can see how listeners might like this stuff. Maybe you can give the man a few props, right?

But then I run smack into a song like "Only the Good Die Young" the upbeat, anti-Catholic teenage rebellion song that your parents and even your grandparents might like, which, of course, makes it the antithesis of a teenage rebellion song. Like "Uptown Girl," it feels bogus and dishonest; it may be a clever hook—one that goes back to Herodotus with "Whom the gods love die young," and recurs with Daniel Defoe ("the good die early, the bad die late'), and later with William Wordsworth ("The good die first")—but trust me, despite what all these smart guys have written, the good are not the only ones who die young. And that dishonesty is troublesome, isn't it? Especially when you consider that one of Billy Joel's biggest hits is called "Honesty." It's a melancholy ballad, and rather cynical. "Honesty is such a lonely word/Everyone is so untrue" goes the first half of the chorus. This, too, is bullshit. A self-pitying singer damning everyone. But perhaps "Honesty" is Joel's most confessional moment about himself and his music.

Joel can't actually write about himself even when he tries to. Give a listen to the monumentally unoriginal "We Didn't Start the Fire" (it is a total rip-off of R.E.M.'s far catchier "It's the End of the World As We Know It," which was a rip-off of—okay, perhaps a salute to—Bob Dylan's "Subterranean Homesick Blues," which was inspired by Chuck Berry's "Too Much Monkey Business"), and it is impossible to offer up any good will toward it. The song is a litany of popular names, major events, titles and places that made headlines during the 40 years of Joel's life leading up to the recording. These tropes are held together by a meaningless chorus of denial about not starting a fire, which apparently was "always burning" even though "we tried to fight it."

I've read these lyrics over and over, and while I get the stream of historical references, the chorus does zero to unify them. What fire? Why did we try to fight it? When did we try? What the fuck is he talking about? I'm going to guess Joel is talking about the passage of time. But there's no way of knowing that unless you know that Joel turning 40 inspired the song. At least R.E.M.'s song, which mashes similar cultural signifiers with rapid-fire rhymes, has a chorus that is bathed in irony, or nihilism, or maybe both. It's a list of inscrutable, stream-of-consciousness phrases and name-dropped figures of the past, and now, according to Michael Stipe's chorus, it's going away—and he feels fine. Or does he really? Irony alert!

So you see the problem, right? Here I am trying my damnedest to rehabilitate Billy Joel, or at least give him his due, and try—TRY—to appreciate his songcraft. But it's not possible. It's not. *Because the craft itself is so often flawed.* His songs fall apart under minimal pressure. Too often with Billy Joel, the melody might sound okay and the phrasing might seem cool, but the lyrics suck or are totally clichéd or noxiously cynical. Or, as my pal Ray says about "New York State of Mind," things move along well, "and then the mawkish sax solo starts." Or the song might *seem* upbeat, but the rhythms are tepid. Or the singing might *seem* impassioned, but you can hear him reaching, acting, placing a fake growl in his voice, say, during "Only the Good Die Young." Too many Joel songs feel like an act. And what is an act? It's fake, it's false. It's artifice not art. It's *inauthentic*. There's no honesty in hearing range, and in the end, we are left like the pathetic narrator of "Honesty"—wishing we could get a taste of the truth, of a song that comes from an artist or from the heart, not from an insincere, uninvested, cynical craftsman trying to ooze earnestness.

Unfortunately, all of this will be lost on Billy Joel fans.

I'm still hoping to reach my son.

# DOES RUSH SUCK? OR THE QUESTION OF TASTE

*Rock fan: Rush's songs stink. They suck.*
*Rush fan: Yeah, I know. But they're really great musicians.*

WE CAN ARGUE ABOUT BEATLES OR STONES, OR WHETHER BILLY Joel deserves our respect, but it is an unassailable fact that Rush is the most controversial band in all of rock.

That's because nobody likes Rush except Rush fans.

That might seem like an obvious statement, but it isn't. There are tons of bands you might like but you would never declare your solemn allegiance to and call yourself a fan of.

I like many of the songs on the Eagles' *Hotel California* album. I think the title track is pretty great. And so is "Life in the Fast Lane." I am, however, not a fan. I've never bought an Eagles album. I don't really know which Eagles member wrote which song. I think the singing on "Witchy Woman" is both impressive and ridiculous. I pretty much detest all of Don Henley's post-Eagles solo work that I've heard. I can't even name all the guys in the band. There's Joe Walsh, Henley, and some key guy plus Timothy B. Schmit—and I'm not even sure what instrument Timothy B. Schmit played. When the Eagles are on the radio, I confuse "Take It Easy" with "Already Gone," and wonder why their greatest hits album sold so many copies.

So I kinda like the Eagles. But I'm not a fan. I would never spend money to see an Eagles show.

Rush fans lionize their favorite band. What does the Rush fan love about Rush? Let's look at the root of the joke that started this essay—their excellent musicianship. Rush is a power trio. A power trio is not the same thing as a regular old trio because a power trio has more—wait for it—power. Power in this case is not just about wattage, although the greatest power trios—Cream, the Jimi Hendrix Experience, ZZ Top—have relied heavily on volume. Power is also about musical density. The power trio lineup of bass, drums and guitar has less sonic padding than the average rock band. There is no keyboard or rhythm guitar filling out the sound. No horn section providing harmonic nuance or rhythmic blasts, no front man or woman entertaining audiences and possibly distracting from the music. Which means that the power trio has license—some might say the need—to fill the space, to play the root and add lots of filigree. To lay down a groove and spare no fills, to solo long, loud, and, eventually, fast.

Filling musical space in this way has many names. Seen in a positive light, this style of play is called displaying chops. Chops equals musical skill—virtuosity. In a dimmer light, displaying chops can be called being busy. When musicians talk about being busy it is usually a nod to musicianship—lots of notes delivered with melodic and harmonic accuracy played at blistering speed is a demonstration of technical skill—but that is not always a good thing. For many listeners, such demonstrations can veer into the world of overplaying. And overplaying can really suck.

Rush is very busy. The band displays its chops with the hallmarks of progressive rock: ornately arranged song structures, shifting time signatures, varying stylistic approaches within the same song, and lots of long solos.

A power trio that doesn't vary it up, or lacks virtuosity, isn't going to get very far. So Rush's M.O. is not without logic. For those who love highly technical rock with complex arrangements, quirky vocals, indulgent solos and lyrics that favor "big ideas" and anti-authoritarian subject matter over love songs, Rush may well be the greatest band in the world.

But for everyone else, these are high crimes and misdemeanors. I have met few, if any, casual admirers of Rush. In fact, I usually never even think of Rush—and you probably don't either, unless you are a devoted fan, a drummer, or are prone to discussing Canadian rock bands. This is not surprising. The case against Rush can and has filled volumes. But let's keep it simple; there are four basic reasons not to like Rush:

1. Geddy Lee's voice
2. Neil Peart's lyrics

3.  Rampant, unabashed, shameless
    self-indulgence
4.  They once called Ayn Rand a genius
    in their liner notes

Lest anyone think I am just flying off the handle here, let's spend a little time on each of these. But as we do, bear in mind that the first three points of anguish are sonic manna for Rush fans.

Geddy Lee, Rush's bassist and vocalist, has a high-pitched voice that might be appreciated in Middle Earth, but has no business being heard on the planet's real continents. Brittle, mildly affected, it is beyond the ken of many listeners and critics. Jon Pareles in *The New York Times* once wrote that Lee's voice "suggests a munchkin giving a sermon." Writing for *Rolling Stone*, Steve Pond compared Lee's "amazingly high-pitched wailing" to "Mr. Bill trying to sing heavy metal." Mr. Bill, for the record, was a claymation character created for a *Saturday Night Live* skit.

In fairness, let the record also show that metal magazine *Hit Parader* once named Geddy Lee Heavy Metal's 13th greatest singer of all time. Rush fans no doubt agree. Redeeming the *Hit Parader* list is the fact that Led Zeppelin's Robert Plant was ranked number one.

Neil Peart is frequently acknowledged as one of rock's great drummers—a stance I don't completely share; while talented, he's largely funkless (In the words of Pareles, "Mr Peart prefers subdivisions to syncopation"). He's also one of its worst lyricists. Peart's lyrics, especially his early sci-fi and mythology-based epics, border on the ridiculous and then cross right into it. This is not to say that Peart, the wear-it-on-his-sleeve reader of books (he blogs his reading list, or used to), isn't writing about worthy things. Often he is, with stilted phrasing, grandiose pomp, and hookless melodies. *Blender* called him the second worst lyricist of all time, beaten out, according to their experts, by that high priest of pop pomposity, Sting. I actually think Peart is worse, but okay. *The Boston Phoenix*, in a piece about rock's worst lyrics, called out the song "Xanadu," which pretentiously cherry-picks from Coleridge's famous "Kubla Khan," its narrator standing "within the Pleasure Dome," finding "the sacred river Alph," dining "on honeydew," and drinking "the milk of Paradise."

Put the overplaying, the pompous lyrics, and the lengthy arrangements together and you have a perfect storm. Rush songs are often masterpieces of self-indulgence and self-importance. How self-indulgent? Their go-for-broke album *2112* features a side-length sci-fi allegory (which defied their record label's expectations by becoming a hit). It also contains this shout-out: "With acknowledgement to the genius of Ayn Rand."

This is a perfect salute for Rush to make, because Ayn Rand, to be polite, is one of the most polarizing "literary"—I use that word lightly—figures of the 20th century. To be impolite, she's one of the nastiest me-first fans of irresponsible capitalism to have ever walked the planet. Her rabidly anti-socialist "philosophy" of "Objectivism" celebrates the individual and pisses on any possibility of a collective good. She was also a windbag of a novelist, with her two grandiose novels clocking in at 1000-plus and 700-plus pages filled with endless monologues. No wonder Rush has trouble writing three-minute pop songs.

In a 1981 interview in *Creem*, Peart said, "Everything I do has Howard Roark in it, you know, as much as anything. The person I write for is Howard Roark."

Howard Roark is the hero of Rand's shorter novel, *The Fountainhead*. He's an *über*architect who is better than you and me.

While it's easy to identify with the anti-authoritarian, pro-individual bent of many Rush lyrics, it's ironic that Rand's odious anti-collectivist philosophy ultimately celebrates power of the few—"geniuses" like Howard Roark, for example—over the many.

Fuck that, him, and her.

Yet there are *millions* of people who love Rush. Which is to say, Rush's music and lyrics appeal to them, to their musical taste.

How is taste different from identity?

Taste can be viewed as a subset of identity. It comes from an established hierarchy of preference and distinctions. We all like guitar solos (and if you don't, why are you reading this book?), but we don't all like all guitar solos. Guitar solos have distinct sounds, tonal, textural qualities, and melodic structures. They have a length, a feel, an attitude, a key. How those elements resonate with listeners helps define taste.

In academic circles, definitions of taste are known as aesthetic sensibilities. These are explorations, if you will, of the qualities that define beauty in music and art. Just who decides these laws is a sticky question.[2] On one level, anyone who interacts with

---

2   The aesthetics of rock are hard to codify—this book is proof of that. One man's beloved Rush is another man's nausea-inducing sonic error. But some brave souls have tried. Two notable books that grapple with what rock is and should be are Richard Meltzer's chaotic and noble *The Aesthetics of Rock*, written in the pre-rock criticism year of 1967. More than two decades later, Joe Carducci, a former mover and shaker for the terrific and influential California punk label SST, wrote *Rock and the Pop Narcotic*, a controversial but cogent look at class divisions that shaped rock and the physical reaction

art brings his or her own definitions to that experience. That said, aesthetic philosophers and music scientists have tried to establish common threads that define "good" or "beautiful" music. And some of these threads are dictated by our brains. There are, for instance, accepted laws of consonance (when sounds go together) and dissonance (when they don't). There are at least two ways sound can overload the brain. The first is neurological dissonance: Our ears' receptors can't handle sounds that are too close together, so playing a C and C-sharp together makes it hard for our brains to separate the frequencies. The second is a rhythmic dissonance. Sound is made of vibrations known as cycles. If two different cycles are vibrating too closely, say, 110 cycles per second and 112 per second, the result is an off-beat, imprecise, chaotic sonic chafing. Brains, generally speaking, don't like this.

The brain also reacts to harmonies, tonality and timbre—the quality of a sound (brash, abrasive, screeching; soothing, robust, beguiling)—but not all brains react the same way. And so here we get back to the issue of Geddy Lee's voice. Why is it considered intrinsically beautiful by some listeners, while for others it conjures up visions of sick elves crooning around a campfire?

The short answer is music isn't exclusively about purity and harmony. And rock 'n' roll sure as hell isn't. Rock is filled with singers who challenge the accepted notions of a "good voice." Bob Dylan's nasal, gruff, and wizened voice has probably annoyed as many listeners as he has inspired. Neil Young's reedy,

---

of "good" rock. Carducci's book is fascinating and well thought out, but it ultimately dismisses pop as an inferior art form. Maybe sometimes, but there is a lot of pop to love.

whining vocals also repel legions. These voices lack the generally accepted clarity, purity, warmth of tone and emotion of a Frank Sinatra, a Marvin Gaye, a Freddie Mercury. But we can love Dylan's and Young's singing because rock 'n' roll is filled with friction and dissonance and edge. And so imperfect voices can lend themselves to rock as long as they are unique and evocative.

The longer answer is that aesthetic rules leave room for us to value other things beyond tonal "purity" or consonance or musicianship. The art of rock songwriting—composition—has generally accepted rules. To certain ears, concision, phrasing, catchy melodies can carry just as much weight as a beautiful tone. Subject matter is a huge aspect of songwriting, especially when it comes to connecting to audiences. Personality and performance are also part of the aesthetic. Is the performer empathetic? Spellbinding? Charismatic? Profound? Pretentious? All those things are part of the musical aesthetic. Is a random audience likely to enjoy and relish a 20-minute disconnected suite about the methods of manufacturing Tupperware performed and sung by a band behind a black curtain? Probably not.

So when Geddy Lee, in his powerful, high voice, sings Neil Peart's lyrics—which only start after "Xanadu's" 5-minute instrumental introduction that moves from noodling to bell chiming to elaborate riffing—about its narrator's Kubla Khan-like search for immortality, why is the song considered laughably bad when compared to, say, Dylan's anthemic "A Hard Rain's A-Gonna Fall," Neil Young's corrosive electric version of "My My, Hey Hey," or the Beatles' rocking-but-fluffy "She Loves You"?

"She Loves You" is as basic as breathing. It is to-the-point, concise, fun, entertaining and has irresistible, candy-coated hooks. "Hey Hey" packs a lyrical and visceral wallop with allusions to punk rock, fame, and death behind thick, stabbing guitar riffs. "Hard Rain" is mysterious, allegorical, poetic. It can be considered pretentious, I suppose, if you get bogged down in the wordplay, except it's rooted in the folk song tradition, which by its nature—for the folk—is not pretentious.

"Xanadu" is not a folk song. It aspires to be an epic, ambitious progressive rock song and as such, it has its moments. But to grasp its full lyrical meaning you need to be familiar with a poem by Samuel Taylor Coleridge, and to do that you have to endure a full complement of windbag, stilted, referential lyrics that will remind you of a nightmarish high school English class. There is a fine line in rock music aesthetics between lyrical depth and pretentiousness. Rush frequently crosses it.

Taste doesn't exist in a vacuum. It is shaped, in part, by the past. As mentioned earlier, studies have shown that the more a listener hears a piece of music, the greater the chance he or she will like it. We can observe this idea—that familiarity breeds for most people, not contempt, but assent—by looking at and listening to Top 40 music.

At a very basic level, a song needs to receive radio airplay in order to receive more airplay. This is because radio stations react to requests (and promotional marketing dollars). The more a song is played and becomes familiar, the more it is requested, and the more it is played. And the cycle continues, until a saturation point is hit, or the demand for other, usually newer, songs pushes the original song aside.

You can hear this familiarity phenomenon at work in a group of Top 40 hits. The sounds of one hit are often echoed in the next; musical trends and sonic movements—doo-wop, Motown, country-rock, disco, grunge—dominate the charts in bunches. In recent years the horrible overuse of autotune, which employs digital wizardry to transform a voice into a robotic warble, or the thickly multi-tracked vocal choruses of songs produced by Dr. Luke for the likes of Katy Perry, Kelly Clarkson, and Pink, are examples of rampant, repetitive replication of familiar sounds that frequently lead to hits. The music audience likes what it already liked.

Taste also is shaped by socioeconomic issues, such as class and peers. We like what we hear, and what we hear is the music played in our communities. But exposure to music that is not part of our community can also shape our taste. Music can be a signifier of class and ethnicity. If we have grown up thinking that other people—say, stuffy, rich white people, for example, like opera and classical music—and we resent those people, we may resent that music, too. But if we are fascinated by stuffy, rich white people, then maybe we will be more open to opera or classical music and embrace it.

But imagine hearing a piece of music with no context? What then? How do we process unfamiliar music without context? How does that fit into taste?

Taste evolves and devolves. It is part of our personality, our identity. And heard-for-the-first-time music can invite multiple reactions. We hear a new piece of music and say, "What is that?"— and if the sound is alien to us, we may not have a frame of reference for it. Some will dismiss a new sound as "noise." A sophisticated or an open-eared listener, however, may rise to the challenge by focusing on the instrumentation, the melodies, the rhythms, the timbre and by checking how these aspects of the alien music make us feel and by looking for similarities to other music. Using these tools of segmentation and compartmentalization, we figure out whether we understand any of the alien music, and whether it appeals to our taste. Which is to say: whether we like it, or are interested in it.

So listening for the first time to anything, whether it's the Velvet Underground, the Beach Boys, Thin Lizzy, or Chuck Berry, the same thing happens: you try to process it.

Bonding over music is a fantastically strong shaper of taste because music goes beyond helping define our identity; it offers a kind of psychic cement between listeners. It's shorthand for liking the same things, for declaring allegiances, finding common ground. When I look back to high school, many of my friends worshipped Pink Floyd and Genesis. I did not share their zeal, but I didn't laugh or mock those bands to my friends. To have done so would have alienated members of a peer group I cared about. I appreciated and celebrated aspects of Pink Floyd and Genesis, and waited until it was my turn to play the Police or Steely Dan or Talking Heads.

When I first heard Rush in a college dorm room in 1981, Geddy Lee's voice and the elaborate arrangements put me off. I had to stifle a laugh, actually. But kids in my dorm—my community—were into it, so I listened and hid my smirk. I didn't really connect with the avowed prog-heads in my dorm. A fan of punk, rock, pop, dance music, and jazz, I didn't connect with Rush. Had those dorm-mates been my pals, I might have made the leap to embrace Rush, or conversely, had I loved Rush, I might have made those dorm-mates my pals. But neither happened. It was a matter of taste.

The brief gag that opens this essay is a riff off this old joke about taste and excess:

> *"The food at this place is terrible," confides a woman to her friend.*
>
> *"I know," agrees the friend, "and the portions are so small!"*

You get it, right? If the friend agrees the food sucks, then why would she want more of it? The same can be asked about a Rush fan: If the music or songs suck, then who cares if the musicians are excellent?

Okay, so maybe it's not a great joke, but it doesn't totally suck, and neither, I guess, does Rush.

Well, actually, that's not true. Rush believes in what they are doing. They have taken chances. They have integrity. They are not cynical schlockmeisters just looking to make a fast buck. They are skilled musicians who play music they love and find interesting and fulfilling, and yet, it does not suit my tastes or that of many other music lovers. I believe, according to my personal taste and critical standards, that they do, in fact, suck, for all the reasons stated earlier. But those reasons will not resonate with Rush fans, who will go on believing Rush does not suck.

I realize this evenhanded, egalitarian, to-each-his-or-her-own perspective regarding taste may strike you as taking the fun and passion out of music criticism. You would be right, and I'm sorry about that. But Rush is to music as liver is to food. Introduced to it at an early age, without the prejudice of accepted critical standards—such as: overplaying is lame, weird time signatures are not inherently cool, pretentious lyrics are not the same as poetic lyrics, and there's nothing wrong with a two-minute and 20-second pop song—it's possible you like the band and don't think they suck. And given your musical DNA, that's perfectly acceptable.

Now, Billy Joel, on the other hand . . .

# WHAT DO YOU CALL A DRUMMER IN A THREE-PIECE SUIT? OR THE QUESTION OF ROCK BAND HIERARCHY

## ANOTHER MORONIC DIALOGUE

*"How can you tell a drummer's at the door?"*

"The knocking speeds up."

*"What's the last thing a drummer says in a band?"*

"'Hey, how about we try one of my songs?'"

*"Why do guitarists put drumsticks on the dashboard of their car?"*

"So they can park in the handicapped spot."

*"How is a drum solo like a sneeze?"*

"You know it's coming, but there's nothing you can do to stop it."

*"What's the first thing a drummer says when he moves to LA?"*

"Would you like fries with that, sir?"

*"What is the difference between a drummer and a savings bond?"*

"One will mature and make money."

*"What did the drummer say to the bandleader?"*

"'Do you want me to play too fast or too slow?'"

# A VERY SHORT FABLE

*Three guys are talking.* "I've got an I.Q. of 139," *brags the first.* "I'm an investment banker and I make $3 million a year."

*"Oh yeah?" says the second, not to be outdone.* "I sold my own software company for $15 million last year. And my I.Q. is 145."

*"You guys are doing pretty good," says the third guy.* "My I.Q. is 85."

*"Really?" ask the two millionaires in unison.* "What kind of drums do you play?"

# A VERY SHORT MORONIC DIALOGUE

*"What do you call a drummer in a three-piece suit?"*

"The defendant."

• • •

# METAPHYSICAL GRAFFITI

This is the chapter where it's time, as James Brown used to order his band, to give the drummer some. The defendant—I mean, drummer—needs someone in his or her corner, because God knows, rock 'n' roll's timekeepers have a serious image problem.

Maybe in West Africa, where I'm guessing master drummers hold honored positions in society, drummers get the respect they deserve. But let's face it, in the world of rock, drummers are usually relegated to a status slightly above that of a roadie.

I should know. I play guitar.

In over three decades of gigging, interviewing musicians, and hanging out with bands in rehearsal studios and backstage, I have heard exactly one singer joke. Here:

> Q. *How many lead singers does it take to change a light bulb?*

> A. *One. The singer holds the light bulb and the world revolves around him.*

That's it. A single singer joke about egotism versus countless gags about drummers, most of which mock timekeepers for being stupid, incompetent, unmusical, witless, or focused to the point of idiocy. Considering that the drummer is arguably the second most crucial member of any rock band—if not *the* most crucial member—this is absurd.

I'm sure many readers are scoffing at that last sentence and wondering who the most important member of a group is. That is easy:

The frontman is the most important member in 99 percent of all rock bands. That is because, ideally, the frontman has the "thing." What is the "thing"? A combination of vocals, looks, and an intangible, unbottle-able blend of charisma and style and musical vision. The "thing"—star quality—is truly rare, which is why most bands and singers suck. One of the problems with the TV show *American Idol* is how few of the contestants— even the winners—have had the "thing." *American Idol* and that other show, *The Voice,* have created the cult of vocal chops, where contestants are largely judged on their singing ability. This is a disservice to rock. A voice is only part of the "thing" that makes a frontman great. Nobody on *American Idol* has had the mesmerizing star quality of James Brown, Tina Turner, Mick Jagger, Amy Winehouse, David Bowie, Robert Plant, David Byrne, Janis Joplin, Madonna, Michael Jackson. None. Zero. It's not even close—the contestants on *American Idol* haven't been frontmen or frontwomen. They were singers.

Interestingly, some of the greatest frontmen in history have not, technically, been great singers. I'm talking about Jonathan Richman of the Modern Lovers, or adenoidal Johnny Rotten of the Sex Pistols. Given their cracking voices and unfashionable timbres, solo rock stars like Dylan and Neil Young probably would never have passed a first audition with the judges of *Amerian Idol.* Ditto Lou Reed or Leonard Cohen.

The frontman is the one who must get the song over. The frontman largely projects and defines a band's image. The frontman, for the average listener, is the band—the man or woman you watch, the king or queen, or, in some cases, court jester, of a band's projected rock 'n' roll fantasy.

There are some bands where the frontman is not the most important member. These are the one percenters of rock. Pete Townshend of the Who is more important than singer Roger

Daltrey when it comes to writing the songs and creating the sound and defining an attitude. Sure, Daltrey is handsome and talented. But he needed Townshend more than the other way around.

AC/DC's fraternal guitarists Angus and Malcom Young (and a third brother who operated behind the scenes) have provided the current that drove that band for decades, while singers changed from Bon Scott to Brian Johnson to Axl Rose. Carlos Santana, too, had a guitar sound that dwarfed his vocalists. And as charming as ABBA singers Agnetha Fältskog and Anni-Frid Lyngstad were, the guys in the background—Björn Ulvaeus and Benny Andersson—turned the group into one of the biggest acts in music history.

But these guys are the exception to the rule.

There is, to be fair, a gray area, where it is hard to say who is the more important force—the frontman or the creative leader? Van Halen is a case in point. Eddie V runs the band. It's got his name, and his record company promoted his guitar virtuosity. He defines the band. That said, to many, the group's initial frontman, the charismatic David Lee Roth, gave the boss a run for the spotlight. To my metal-ignorant ears, Roth, a preening master of campy rock excess, personified the fun, outrageous virtuosity of the band. I enjoyed watching him far more that watching his bandmate tapping on strings and making whammy bar squeals.

More commonly, though, the frontman trumps the auteur, at least in the mind of the public. Take Fleetwood Mac or No Doubt. Lindsey Buckingham may have powered the genius of *Rumours*, but Stevie Nicks was the face of the band. Gwen

Stefani, who initially joined No Doubt as a backup singer, didn't write most of the band's early music. But it didn't take long for her look and voice to define the band for most people. She was the alpha female.

Drummers not named Phil Collins and Neil Peart don't write many songs, generally speaking, and they don't sing much either. But while many great singers—Dylan, Young, Jonathan Richman, Johnny Rotten—are technically lousy, a band with a really crappy drummer is unlistenable. That's because the drums are the engine of rock. So listening to a crappy drummer is as fun as driving a car that keeps stalling. Most bands suck, for any of three reasons: the material sucks, the singer sucks or the drummer sucks.

The only record I like with really bad drumming is *The Langley Schools Music Project,* a collection from the '70s featuring school kids covering songs, like "Space Oddity" and "Desperado." Most of the kids can't quite master their instruments, but that is what makes the album so endearing and moving: the friction of their youthful sincerity and their musical clunkers.

Not mastering the drums in rock is understandable given that playing the drums is fucking hard. To play them well, you've got to be able to play four separate rhythms *at the same time* and keep the root tempo steady. Remember when you were a kid and someone challenged you to rub your tummy in a circle and pat your head at the same time? It was difficult, right? Imagine having to reverse the direction of your rub after each cycle, tapping your head twice after the first rub and once after the second, while hopping on one foot and kicking out with your other foot after every three hops.

# METAPHYSICAL GRAFFITI

Go on, try it.
You look ridiculous.

DESPITE SUCH A REMARKABLE SKILL SET, THE DRUMMER IN rock circles is almost *never* automatically regarded as a magician, a priest, or even the engine that drives the machine. The drummer, by and large, is derided, mocked, and pissed on in the world of rock.

Why is this?

There are a number of theories. A friend of mine who is a drummer and who I know to be extremely smart and creative, says the stigma of drumming starts in high school band.

"If you have no discernible talent on any of the chair instruments," he says, "they stick you in the drum section. The logic is that even the biggest moron could knock out a beat on a wood block or triangle."

*How many drummers does it take to change a light bulb?*

*Four. One to change the lightbulb and three to discuss how Neil Peart would have done it.*

Ironically, drummers are often perceived as dummies but they are also derided for being focused and devoted to their art. The light bulb gag is partly about drummers being overanalytical and partly about being obsessed with style and technique. Drummers may be the geekiest of all players in rock. They love to talk shop—discussing equipment and other drummers. Perhaps the nerdiest thing about drummers and drumming, though, is the name for the stool they sit on: the "throne." Listen, I'm here advocating for drummers and yet, it's hard to say drum throne with a straight face. Note to drummers: If that's a throne, the kingdom must be in pretty bad shape.

Drummers are so into drums they actually go to clinics. No, these are not places where sick people go for treatment; drum clinics are places of instruction. Drummers who want to get better, who equate great chops with great music, flock to clinics. And more power to them. But on another level going to a clinic violates one of the unspoken rules of rock—make it look easy and effortless.

No doubt Jimi Hendrix logged plenty of hours, days, weeks, and months playing scales and honing his moves and sounds. And the same goes for every other guitar god out there. But nobody ever thinks of little Jimmy Page slaving away in his tiny English bedroom trying to master his chords and scales. Yes, these guys were geniuses who no doubt displayed remarkable chops at a young age. But they got good behind closed doors. The truth is rock stars only *seem* to spring to the stage fully formed and ready to rock! They practice a lot. But not in public.

Yes, there are musical obsessives for all instruments. Guitarists study finger-picking styles, theorize about guitar strings, and worship certain brands. Keyboardists—particularly the technology fans I think of as "midiots"—love their gear, too. But drummers—and yes, there are exceptions—are a breed apart.

THERE ARE OTHER REASONS DRUMMERS ARE SCORNED BY THEIR fellow musicians. These usually have to do with a drummer's musical identity and playing style. Playing with someone who hits his drums with the force of a sledgehammer and is relentlessly loud can suck. But it also sucks when you play with a light-wristed jazzophile who refuses to bring the big beat when the rest of the band wants to rock out. Meanwhile, drummers who are into musical complexity at the expense of the song are just fucking annoying. These are the guys who seem more into math ("let's play in 7/8 time and then switch to 11/13!") than music. Drummers who are into ego-boosting fills and solos are also annoying.

So some of the jokes are borne out of real-life archetypes and possibly a thirst for revenge. Drummers have the most equipment, which takes up the most room on stage, and they take the longest to set up and break down. The rest of the band—and I'm talking about every band ever—hates them for it.

Musicians aren't the only ones who beat up on drummers. Pop culture gets in on the act, too. The stereotyping starts early: In *The Muppets*, Animal is an out-of-control wild man. There's a *SpongeBob SquarePants* episode where Patrick, the titular character's lovably idiotic pal, plays the drums. Burger-obsessed Jughead played the drums in the TV cartoon *The Archies*. The Monkees' drummer Micky Dolenz split clueless-joke duties with Peter Tork.

In the brilliant rock 'n' roll comedy *This Is Spinal Tap*, drummers not only come off as idiots (one dies from choking on *someone else's* vomit), but expendable and replaceable. Spinal Tap drummers are irrelevant except as a punch line; they die—by exploding or choking—but the band goes on.

Sadly, some of the blame for the drummer-as-laughingstock lies with some of rock's most famous practitioners. Leading the charge, of course, is Ringo Starr. Me? I think Ringo is one of the greatest drummers in history, an egoless pro who served on some of the greatest songs ever recorded and NEVER, EVER overplayed. So all you haters out there, all the smarmy drum clinicians who idolize mathematical speed freak players, all the cynics who have railed against Ringo and called him the luckiest, least talented man on earth, guess what? Shame on you. You are beyond wrong.

Still, Ringo's egoless quality has probably hurt the drummer identity more than it's helped. The lovable Liverpudlian wasn't the good-looking Beatle, he didn't write many songs, and the ones Lennon and McCartney let him sing were usually silly. On screen he came across as likably goofy in *A Hard Days Night* and *Help!* And considering he once—during the height of Beatlemania, no less—seriously told an interviewer he wanted to be a hairdresser if things didn't work out with music, he came off as a real-life goofball.

But Ringo can hardly take all the blame for drummers' bad reputation. Not when you had guys like Keith Moon, Ginger Baker, and John Bonham creating a template for creative genius, self-destruction, and total unreliability. Taken individually, those drummers often acted like disgraceful idiots. Add them together, and they come off an informal psychopathic movement.

ULTIMATELY, THE HIERARCHY OF BANDS FOLLOWS THE MONEY. The front person and the songwriter are generally what make or break a band. They are the ones fans relate to, who record companies invest in, who media want to interview and write about. Not the guy in the back you can't even see, and is frequently replaced by a machine. The singer makes the band. The voice is what we react to. The song and video make the band, too. The guitarists can help. From Santana to Van Halen, plenty of bands have been built around guitarists. Drummers? No enduring rock band (as opposed to jazz outfits, where drummers have been legendary band leaders) has ever been formed around a drummer. And yes, I know about the Dave Clark Five and Ginger Baker's Air Force and Genesis. These are weak exceptions to the rule that drummers are replaceable. They can explode, and Spinal Tap will find another.

But even though drummers are replaceable, they also are not.

Playing with lousy drummers is just an awful experience. It kills rock. The early B-52s, Sleater-Kinney, White Stripes, Black Keys, and Yeah Yeah Yeahs have all proved you don't need a bassist to rock. Little Richard and Jerry Lee Lewis proved that, somehow, you don't even need a guitar to rock. And we all know if you have a guitar, a keyboard is never required. But no drums? Well, there are performers—Jimi Hendrix, Richie Havens, Richard Thompson, and even, I suppose, Ed Sheeran, who can rock without them for a while—but it's not something anyone should make a habit of.

A good drummer is the blood, the water, the chi, the force that makes rock roll.

And a good drummer that can carry on a conversation about current events and knows how to read?

Priceless.

# ROCK'S SECRET WEAPON, OR THE QUESTION OF AUDACITY (AND CONCEPT ALBUMS)

WHAT IS IT ABOUT GREAT ROCK MUSIC THAT GETS US TO LISTEN, TO dance and sing along, to become fans, to pledge our undying allegiance, to follow a band obsessively, to buy books about the bands we love, or—never mind spending time reading those books—to actually devote hours, days, weeks and years to writing them in the first place?

Crazy, right?

There are a number of answers to this question. Or perhaps I should say factors. They are obvious and many of them have already been touched on in previous chapters: A song or band or album appeals to your identity. Music has a great hook or melody or lyric that fits your taste for whatever reason. It's sexy and wild. Or, as the primal, anti-intellectual critics among us concisely say: "It's got a good beat and you can dance to it."

I submit one factor is more vital than all the others.

But to get at this quality, I'm going to turn to literature for a few paragraphs, and specifically, Philip Roth, my pick for America's greatest post-World War II novelist.

Don't worry. It'll be fun. Even though Roth is a guy given to listening to and extolling the transcendent virtues of the string quartet, he is arguably the most rock 'n' roll writer in American history. He has written about sex, America, baseball, Jews, politics, and race in frank, honest, hilarious, outrageous, and moving ways. If you think the Sex Pistols were shocking in their name, attitudes, and nihilism, they have nothing on Roth, who was a punk before punk. Not in a music or fashion sense, of course, but in the fearlessness and passion of his work. His short story "Defender of the Faith" shocked Jews with the portrayal of a wheedling Army man who appeals to a senior officer for special treatment because they are both members of the tribe. His novel *Portnoy's Complaint* shocked everyone with its blunt, hilariously frank embrace of sexual obsession. In one tears-of-laughter-inducing tale, his hero Alexander Portnoy recalls his teenaged self masturbating into a piece of liver he has taken from the icebox and then, once violated, returning it to the fridge. Later, he witnesses the soiled piece of meat cooked and served to his family.

Top that, Johnny Rotten!

Years later, in *Sabbath's Theater*, Roth's anti-hero Mickey Sabbath visits the grave of his great love to spill his seed upon her burial site—and finds a romantic rival doing the very same thing.

But Roth's greatest contribution to understanding the power of rock 'n' roll has nothing to do with outrageous gags involving self-abuse. It comes from his novel *I Married a Communist*, which contains a vital lesson about writing and about criticism. And it is this lesson that can be applied to rock.

*I Married a Communist* centers on the recollections of Nathan Zuckerman, a frequent Roth narrator. This time out, Nathan recounts the life of his one-time idol, Ira Ringold, a strapping man who becomes the hero of a popular radio drama about labor hero Iron Rinn. Young Nathan meets the proletarian star—his teacher is Ira's brother—and at one point they begin to discuss a Thomas Paine quote about King George that they both admire: "I should suffer the misery of devils, were I to be a whore of my soul by swearing allegiance to one whose character is that of a sottish, stupid, stubborn, worthless, brutish man."

Ira asks Nathan why he likes the quote, and they discuss the phrase "whore of my soul." Nathan concludes it's more powerful than saying, "were I to sell my soul." And he explains to Ira:

> *People don't go around writing 'whore' in public, saying 'whore.'"*
> *"Why don't they?"*
> *"Shame. Embarrassment. Propriety."*
> *"Propriety. Good. Right. So this is audacious, then."*
> *"Yes."*
> *"And that's what you like about Paine, isn't it. His audacity!"*
> *"I think so. Yes."*
> *"And now you know why you like what you like. ... you saw right through that word, saw through it*

> *as through a magnifying glass, to one of the*
> *sources of this great writer's power. He*
> *is audacious. Thomas Paine is audacious. But is*
> *that enough? That is only a part of the formula.*
> *Audacity must have a purpose, otherwise it's cheap*
> *and facile and vulgar..."*

And there you have it: Audacity is rock's secret weapon (not to mention one of Roth's). What is audacity? Dictionaries offer two meanings. The first is "the willingness to take bold risks," and the second is "rude, disrespectful behavior." In many instances, that second definition is an intrinsic part of the first. Taking bold risks challenges orthodoxy, and challenging orthodoxy is, at least to those who adhere to the status quo, often perceived as rude and disrespectful. The word is similar to another term often associated with rock, rebellion—the act of resisting authority or convention—but without its willful opposition. Being audacious isn't simply saying "no" to something; it's actively, creatively saying yes to something else.

At its root, then, rock 'n' roll is an audacious art form. From its earliest R&B incarnations it was louder, more provocative, and more aggressive than what had gone before. It was sexier, dirtier and funnier, too. The pioneers of rock, Louis Jordan, Big Joe Turner, and others, offered witty and wicked double-entendred fun with a big beat. ("I'm like a one-eyed cat, peepin' in a seafood store," shouts Big Joe, letting two sexually charged metaphors fly in "Shake, Rattle & Roll.")

Later, Elvis Presley encapsulated and enhanced that beat with a few pelvic thrusts. Meanwhile, in New Orleans, Esquerita and Little Richard would bring outrageous—for its time—androgyny to the art form. The audacity expanded from sound and words and dance into clothing and style; there were rockers and greasers and mods, and then, eventually the Beatles had the audacity to morph from adorable mop tops to shaggy hippies.

But rock's audacity wasn't just confined to sound or sex or style. The elastic superpower of audacity allows rock itself to morph and grow. The kind of music, the instrumentation, the sound of the recordings and the subject matter of the songs are all up for grabs, thanks to audacity.

THERE HAVE BEEN MANY AUDACIOUS ACTS AND MOMENTS AND records in rock 'n' roll history: dirty ditties of hokum blues, Little Richard and his flamboyant stage persona, Chuck Berry's duck walk and "My Ding-a-Ling" lyrics, Elvis and his pelvis, the Beatles, Dylan going electric, the Stones, the very idea of Woodstock, Jimi Hendrix reinventing the electric guitar and "Star Spangled Banner," the Velvet Underground blending noise and psychedelia, the costumes of Kiss, the Sex Pistols, the idealism and militancy of Minor Threat, the brazen plagiarism and inventiveness of the Sugar Hill Gang, the sci-fi androgyny of David Bowie, the drama of Jim Morrison and the Doors, the excess of Parliament-Funkadelic, the violence and ambition of the Who, the expanded version of Talking Heads, the speed and rage of Husker Du, the political lyrics and moxie of Public Enemy, the sexual sloganeering of Frankie Goes to Hollywood, the sexuality of Madonna, the kookiness of Bjork, the major-label subversion of the Mekons, the visionary sound of My Bloody Valentine. Many of the names on that short list had unique, often outrageous stage personas that made them instantly noticeable. But many had audacious musical ideas. The best of them had both.

The concept album—a thematically linked group of songs on an album—arose in the mid-'60s. The Beatles, with *Sgt. Pepper* and *Magical Mystery Tour*, experimented with loosely linked ideas on an album.[3] Frank Zappa's band, the Mothers of Invention, as well as the Kinks, Small Faces, the Pretty Things, and even Simon & Garfunkel on *Bookends*, explored the idea that an album could be more than a random collection of songs.

On the surface, it doesn't seem like a tremendously radical idea. Song cycles, musicals, and operas—all unified art works of lyric and music—had been around for centuries. And Woody Guthrie's Dust Bowl Ballads collection, though not a rock album, was a notable thematic release back in 1940.

But looking at those early concept albums in a four-year period from 1966 to 1969, we see purposeful, widely different experimentation. Early concept albums were audacious in their ambition, in breaking the cookie-cutter song mold that dominated pop music.

Writing songs with extended narratives or subject matter beyond love, broken hearts, and dancing was a rarity.

So the first concept albums—*The Kinks Are the Village Green Preservation Society*, a song cycle examining British life; Small Faces' *Ogden's Nut Gone Flake*, with a parody album cover and second side devoted to a psychedelic fable about a guy looking

---

3 There are those who classify the Beach Boys' *Pet Sounds* as a concept album. But as far as I can tell, the only concept was for Brian Wilson to ditch the rest of his band and write an entire album of exquisite songs with a few collaborators helping on the lyrics. No doubt Wilson was going on a personal journey while making the album, but I don't hear a unifying concept or narrative.

for the missing half of the moon; and the Pretty Things' *S.F. Sorrow,* a 1968 rock opera (sorry, Who worshippers, your heroes weren't the first[4]) based on a short story—joined *Sgt. Pepper* in elevating the pop and rock album into the realm of "art." That's pretty audacious.

DESPITE OWING A NOD TO THE PRETTY THINGS, THE WHO HAD the audacity to write two very good rock operas, *Tommy* and *Quadrophenia* (three if you count Pete Townshend's *Lifehouse* project)—and the exposure and success of these efforts opened the floodgates. The results of these enterprises varied. The best were inspired and creative and artful. The worst were often described with an adjective—pretentious—that is the failed cousin of calculated audacity.

The difference between audacious rock 'n' roll and pretentious rock 'n' roll is in the ear of the beholder, to some degree. But it is a fact progressive rock bands love concept albums. And from where I sit, that is usually a very bad combination. I've already delved into the problems of progressive rock while writing about Rush, and how prog fundamentally lends itself to charges of pretentiousness. When you combine progressive rock with the concept album—bombastic, self-indulgent music with bombastic, self-indulgent ideas—you risk detonating an explosive chain reaction of pretentiousness. The results can be deadly.

---

4   Not to beat on the Who, but *S.F. Sorrow* contains a song called "Old Man Going," which begins with wickedly fast guitar-strumming—and you can practically sing the lyrics of the Who's "Pinball Wizard" to the song without missing a beat. You could look it up.

Which brings us to Jethro Tull's *Thick as a Brick*, a progressive rock concept album so good, it breaks the prog-rock cycle and even transcends the overuse of flute—perhaps my least favorite instrument in rock.[5]

Despite these obvious strikes against it, *Thick as a Brick* is a work of genius. It's the wolf that would eat Genesis' *The Lamb Lies Down on Broadway*, the sunshine missing from *The Dark Side of the Moon*, and yet it has plenty in common with each. While it took audacity for the likes of Pink Floyd and Genesis to write material that ignored 3-minute-pop song conventions, Jethro Tull's leader, Ian Anderson, beats those groundbreakers at their own game, creating an album comprising one single song. *Thick as a Brick* is arguably rock's first great meta-album. Yes, Zappa and the Mothers of Invention dabbled in the form, from *Cruising with Ruben and the Jets* all the way to *Joe's Garage*, and even *Sgt. Pepper* grazed—barely—the subject of the rock band, but *Thick as a Brick* is a parody, a piss-take, an answer record, and a master stoke of progressive rock—as awesome and dramatic as it is funny.

For those who don't know the backstory, Anderson, the flute-flaunting frontman of the band, wrote the album after critics misinterpreted Tull's previous disc, *Aqualung*, as a concept album. This apparently pissed Anderson off, and he decided he would show everyone how a "real" concept is done. I have no idea

---

5   As a rule, I abhor rock flute. (For anyone wondering, exceptions can be made for War's song "Low Rider," which contains enough cowbell to work as an antidote for this unrock instrument. Also, lest there be any confusion, the wind instruments that accompany "Stairway to Heaven" are not flutes; they are recorders. And, yes, I've heard Rahsaan Roland Kirk, but jazz flute constitutes a whole other book, as any fan of Will Ferrell's hard-blowing *Anchorman* character Ron Burgundy knows.)

if Anderson had even heard the term post-modernism, or read Vladimir Nabokov's great lit-crit lampoon *Pale Fire*, or was aware of meta-fiction. But the album he spat out touches all those bases.

The defiant attitude starts with a caustic and dismissive declaration in the opening lyric: "Really don't mind if you sit this one out." According to the "concept" here—laid out in the form of a news article on the cover—the album lyrics are from a poem written by 8-year-old Gerald (Little Milton) Bostock. The epic poem, according to the article, had won Little Milton a prize from the Society for Literary Advancement and Gestation (SLAG), but was rescinded after a panel of "leading child psychologists" determined the poet was "unbalanced" and his poem revealed "an extremely troublesome attitude toward life, his God and Country."

The deadpan rendering of the story line—which includes a shot of the grim-faced little boy—provides the entire "concept" Anderson needs. The resulting poem is a bile-filled screed that entertains as it insults. And the hostility is couched—cushioned, no, wrapped in silk—in the song's sweetly sung, lilting chorus that declares "You wise men don't know how it feels/to be thick as a brick."

"Thick" in this case is not a measurement of density, it's a synonym for stupidity. Being thick, of course, is an expression for boneheadedness.

And so I believe Anderson's epic—written to show rock savants what a concept is—is an attack. Wise men—music critics, anyone?—aren't so smart, goes Tull's epic; they aren't even aware of being stupid.

But enough of pointing fingers at my fellow music writers. We're all human, except for maybe Lester Bangs. Let's turn back to that Philip Roth excerpt. "Audacity needs a purpose," says Iron Rinn, "otherwise it's cheap and facile and vulgar."

A lot of rock 'n' roll audacity is driven by braggadocio. Rap has is built largely on audacity—outrageous tales of violence, sex and drugs. Bluesmen couldn't resist the tall—or dirty—tale, and neither can certain strains of country (did the devil really go down to Georgia?). And metal, with its ultra-violence, has a high bullshit quotient, too.

True story: I was on a trek in the East African bush, accompanied by an American tour leader and his Samburu tribesmen buddies. As we hiked, our guides would break into song. And sometimes the other tribesmen would laugh at the singer. When I asked what they were singing, the tour leader said, "Usually they sing about what great warriors they are. It's mostly bullshit."

I'm not sure if anyone has studied the connection between singing and audacity. But when a person sings, the brain releases endorphins, pleasure-releasing hormones, and oxytocin, which has been linked to the reduction of stress and anxiety. In this way it is not too much of a stretch—for me, anyway—to say singing can liberate the singer from reality, unleashing the power to brag, to separate from the self or to create another self. (Kinda like writing, but I digress.) Just think about opera and musicals. Singing is a liberating phenomenon; it intrinsically helps the listener and the singer suspend disbelief.

*Thick as a Brick* wasn't an indulgent ego boost, however. It was an album with many goals—to lampoon, to captivate and entertain, to rock, to soothe, to dazzle. And that first quality, that satirizing element, gives it an extra boost because most concept albums have been humorless. And they have suffered for it.

Musically, Jethro Tull turns in a remarkable performance. The album is a single 43-minute and 36-second song that moves between gorgeous folk and medieval settings and venomously hard-rocking riffs and back again. The flute solos are excellent, too.

As I've noted, some listeners will doubtless find transcendent joy in complex music, pretentious lyrics, and overlong solos. I'm sure there's a sense of transgression—audacity!—that comes with willfully ignoring the classic concision of the 2-minute, 30-second pop song structure. Call it the perverse thrill of pomposity.

*Thick as a Brick* takes this flaunting to an extreme, given it's an entire album. This problematic, anti-commercial form must have just added to Ian Anderson's joy. It's the aural equivalent of giving a glitter-wrapped finger to critics and rival artists while wowing and winking to fans. That irreverence, that moxie, helps makes it progressive rock's most enjoyable and ambitious concept album, one that extends the form, playfully, dramatically. It's the most compelling argument for progressive rock I know. And a fine example of rock's—hell, art's—secret weapon.

# GODOT, THE MUSICAL, OR THE QUESTION OF HYPE

IT'S TRUE: ALLEGORIES AND FABLES DON'T USUALLY PRESENT themselves in the form of musicals. And the rock musical is in many ways a contradiction in terms—the music never seems to actually rock when it's in a theater, often a victim of the need for clear lyrics, an older, hearing-challenged audience, and unfriendly (for rock) acoustics. But as the musical *Hamilton* evidently proves (I haven't seen it), rap's focus on words, the flow and killer beats make it theater-friendly. So I have hope that one day this masterpiece of existential drama will live on the Great White Way...

# GODOT, THE MUSICAL

*A tree.*

*A country road.*

*Two men stand motionless in badass B-boy poses. Didi wears cracked sunglasses and giant cracked golden dollar sign pendant. Gogo's oversized football jersey is ripped. Both men wear weathered hats.*

*A thunderous hip-hop beat. They don't move.*

TOGETHER:    Let me hear ya say G-LOVE! ....
                    G-LOVE! ....
                    G-LOVE! ....
                    Let me hear ya say PARTAY! ....
                    PARTAY! ....
                    PARTAY! ....

*They become animated. Stumbling and stalking the stage.*

DIDI:       Yo G-Nation, feel anticipation,
              We ain't the fever, we the inflammation
              Waitin' here for the holy boss
              Think of this as the pregame coin toss.

GOGO:      Gogogogo! The fun has begun
              G ain't here, but I'm like his son.
              They call me Gogo, cause I get things goin'

# METAPHYSICAL GRAFFITI

The crew ain't new, y'all be knowin'
Didi, mah homey, always chillin' wit me,
King dawg Pozzo wit his boy Lucky.

DIDI: Yesterday we was sent on stage
rocking like we always did back in the day
the crowd was feelin' it. Gogo was wheelin it,
The rhymes was crisp like KFC
had deep-fried the motherfucking OED.

GOGO: But the show to remember was not to be
In fact things turned quite nasty
as we got word
the master G would not be heard.
And when we told the crowd he would not
show up
it's like we kicked 'em in the nuts.

*Didi and Gogo cover their groins.*

GOGO: Okay, peeps, this is where I turn bluer
than Two Live Crew or
a sea that's azure.

DIDI: Man, that's some manure!
MY words can delight or cause a huge fright
like when Donald Trump won election night.

GOGO: Now we shock you, now we rock you,
See, G's the one you flock to,

The story you're about to hear is totally true
My boy Didi was chillin' by a tree
Guess what he was sayin'?
He'll tell you for free:

DIDI: WOE IS ME!

GOGO: Didi was complainin' 100 miles an hour
I wanted to pulverize him, like turnin' wheat to flour,
I said, damn, I'm homeless, I got no wealth
Maybe I should just go hang myself
And Didi, he shut up, payin' full attention, he say

DIDI: Yeah, son, we would get an erection!

*Lucky appears stage right, a rope around his neck.*

LUCKY: Quaquaquaqua.

DIDI: GOGO!

GOGO: DIDI!

TOGETHER: We always funnin', a road, a tree!

GOGO: Now some say G stands for Gesus.

DIDI: Yo, don't dismiss him with some stupid alias.

GOGO:     Godot got more flow than the
          motherfuckin' Yangtze,
          Nile, Hudson or the ugly Mississippi.
          When he raps, those rivers run backwards,
          cats stop chasin' birds and MC's forget words,

*LUCKY moves further into the stage. POZZO appears, holding the rope.*

GOGO:     Yo, It's my man Pozzo and his boy Lucky!
          Damn I was wonderin' where they be,
          I can rock the mic 365—
          But a hypeman needs sidekicks to truly thrive.

DIDI:     So cut to Pozzo, let him kick it live.

POZZO:    I'm blind! I need help
          And don't tell me to look it up on Yelp.
          Life is shite
          when you can't see the light.

GOGO:     That's cause it's nearin' round midnight.

POZZO:    Who are you? Violent attackers?
          Scammers, thieves, or candy rappers?

DIDI:     Whoa, whoa, this can't be!
          We met yesterday. There was a road, a tree.

POZZO:    Nah, nah, don't ring a bell.

GOGO:   You had swell.
        You were there. Lucky, too
        Now you look like a party raved you.

POZZO:  Stop busting rhymes for this stupid zoo.
        Get me help or I'm through!

DIDI:   Yo' Pozzo, Don't be dissin' the crowd.
        Gogo been stokin' 'em, gettin' 'em loud.

POZZO:  I don't care, I ain't proud,
        And Gogo got the cred of Turin's shroud.

GOGO:   Pozzo, lemme break it down:
        it ain't sound makin' G frown.
        You go from hangin' around,
        To lost, not found.

*POZZO starts pulling Lucky away.*

GOGO:   Nah, Pozzo, I'm just playin' ya.
        A hypeman jam, flim-flam iamb.
        Every sound tasted, no syllable wasted.
        With my verbal mace did you get faced-ed?

DIDI:   Oh Gogo, You didn't.

GOGO:   I did.

LUCKY:  Quaquaquaqua.

# METAPHYSICAL GRAFFITI

GOGO:      GOGO!

DIDI:      DIDI!

ALL:      We always funnin'! A road, a tree!

*POZZO pulls LUCKY off stage.*

GOGO:      Godot so chill he make Ciudad Juárez
               seem safe like Mecca or Benares.
               He's crucial, elemental, existential.

DIDI:      When I rap about him people think I'm mental.

*DIDI looks stage right. There is a boy, age 10, at the edge of the stage.*

DIDI:      Yo' who's this boy stage right.
               Look like Justin Bieber on Halloween Night.
               Hey, Shorty, dressed so neat
               Like them human kids on *Sesame Street*.

BOY:      Mr. Gogo, I interrupt the show.
               The Master G sent me here to blow:
               You are the clown prince, but it don't
               make sense
               for him to drop by while you rock wit nonsense.

GOGO:      Yo, Lil' Justin, that's one for the dust bin.
               Look at dem peeps on seats being freaks.

They goin' crazy 'cause, our rhymes ain't lazy,
our images ain't hazy, no words can faze me.

DIDI:        Unlike that mom of Stacy!

GOGO:     So you sayin G ain't playin' cause we rock too
good?
I can't handle it, I'm like a vandal that
steals the show then wants to give it back.
Tell Mr G he gotta come,
see the good me and Didi done.
We gettin' tired, we gettin' hoarse
but we always cheer lead with righteous force:

*Boy leaves stage.*

TOGETHER:  We can't go on!
We go on!
We can't go on!
We go on!

*The music stops. Gogo and Didi continue to dance on the stage.*

TOGETHER: We can't go on!
We go on!
We can't go on!
We go on!

*Didi and Gogo return to their original, frozen, badass poses.*

*No one moves.*

GODOT, THE MUSICAL IS, OF COURSE, A TWISTED, INADEQUATE retelling of Samuel Beckett's play *Waiting for Godot*. If you have seen or read this play, chances are that happened a few years or decades ago, so here's a very brief recap: Two down-and-out bums, Vladimir and Estragon, are waiting for a guy named Godot to come, although we never find out who, exactly, Godot is. While they wait, Pozzo and his strange, stuttering, slave-like servant, Lucky, come by. They talk, take their leave, but come back later. A boy appears and tells them Godot won't be coming.

Critics and scholars have interpreted the original work in all kind of ways. It's an absurdist play. It examines the meaning of life. It predates *Seinfeld* as the original show about nothing. It's a political allegory to some, although exactly what nation or geopolitical situation is the root of the supposed allegory depends on the critic reading the play. To others, the two-act marvel is packed with Christian references, or so I'm told.

Fueling all this free-for-all of interpretation is Beckett's minimalist approach—his stage instructions are spare. The narrative, such that it is, remains vague and enigmatic. And Beckett, in a gift to critics and students everywhere, shed very little light when it came to explaining his mysterious work.

The last time I read *Godot*, I was stunned how much its central characters Vladimir and Estragon—who call each other Gogo and Didi—reminded me of hype men. I wanted to see Flavor Flav, who I think of as rap's primo hype man, cast as Estragon in a future restaging.[6]

---

6   Beckett, it's safe to say, would not approve of my vision. He threatened to take director JoAnne Akalaitis to court to stop her from setting his play *Endgame* in a subway station and adding music by Philip Glass. In the end,

I'm serious—the whole play is powered by the idea of an arrival, a meeting that is going to take place. And the G-man is, evidently, hugely important. We never learn what he does. But he's the show, the mack, the star. It says so in the title: *Waiting for Godot.*

The hype man in rap functions as an MC, a warmup and, in the case of Flavor Flav's role in Public Enemy, a clownish sidekick. And he isn't just a sidekick. He's a comic foil.

I like to image Gogo and Didi as humble barkers—guys a few steps removed from the hype men of carnival shows who loudly and brashly declaim about the incredible, enthralling, once-in-a-lifetime, never-before-seen exhibits and shows, hoping to lure the price of admission out of anyone walking by.

Or maybe they are poorly dressed advance men. Or publicists. Or marketers.

All these terms are dedicated to hype. And what is hype? The word seems to be rooted in "hyper," which means "over" or "an increase, to excess." But it may also come from a shortening of the word hyperbole, which means exaggeration. Some dictionaries posit the word may have links to drugs, evolving, it's been theorized, from the hypodermic needle used to shoot heroin.

Whatever the origin, the general meaning of the word hype eventually morphed into "excessive or misleading advertising," according to one etymology dictionary. So hype is, in a word, bullshit.

But a hype man, in the context of rap concerts, isn't spinning bullshit—right? The rap hype man exists to blow trumpets and

---

a settlement was reached in which the programs and ads for the play carried the author's denunciation of the production.

herald the genius that is about to grace the stage. He may be spewing bullshit, but it's bullshit he wants treated as the truth.

Rock 'n' roll has been built on hype on all sides. If audacity is rock's secret primary weapon, then hype is its reusable big bang. It has been there since the beginning, after all. Its early critics issued panicked warning shots, heralding its intrinsic dangers, while its early backers spun the big beat and talked hot and heavy about its powers. DJ Moondog, Alan Freed, the man credited with coining the term "rock 'n' roll," was rock's original hype man. And his radio show was, like the records he played, provocative—at least, for its time. He spoke over records, he hit a cowbell, he thumped out the beat on a phone book. This was radical, shock jock stuff for the early 1950s. He also held Moondog's Coronation Ball in Cleveland in 1952— pretty much the first thousand-seat rock 'n' roll concert—and hyped the show with a poster billing the event as "The most terrible ball of them all."

The hype in this case actually lived up to its name: Fans bum-rushed the show, "knocking down four panel doors," according to the next day's *Cleveland Plain Dealer*, and cops shut down the concert at the jam-packed 9,000-seat Cleveland Arena. "The fire department opened up hoses on the crowd," according to the son of one of the promoters.

Meanwhile, the fear surrounding rock 'n' roll from the law and order establishment on down was equally overblown. Crazy J. Edgar Hoover ordered his FBI to put Freed under surveillance. Rock 'n' roll was a national threat.

Not that J. Edgar was completely wrong. Thanks to 20/20 hindsight, there's little doubt rock has ruined lives—glamorizing drug abuse, providing the soundtrack to rebellion, unwanted pregnancy and STDs for millions intoxicated by the sound and images of rock. But it has also saved kids, including me, from dying of boredom or hopelessness. It made us interested in lyrics, in writing, in reading, social movements, in history, in playing instruments. It gave us, and continues to give millions of others, meaning.

It's also given work to so many, creating entire niche industries. Never mind the bollocks of rock criticism, there are rock-related jobs in everything from fashion, radio, video, T-shirts, concerts, drug paraphernalia, catering, transport, and digital innovation, including that instrument that blurs hipness and hype: social media.

When does hip cross the line into hype? What are the tipping points? If hype is exaggerated and overblown sensationalism, hip is the gestational state before hype. The phrase "I'm hip" is about awareness, about being in the know.

Yet, the state of being hip—being a hipster—has largely been derided. It's hard to understand exactly where the scorn lies. If we define a hipster as someone who follows trends, music, and fashion that are outside the mainstream—what is the harm of that? In science, technology, geography, and so many other disciplines, looking for new ideas is applauded.

But the hatred of the hipster has been around for over half a century. At a minimum. In 1957, feminist Caroline Bird wrote an essay in *Harper's Bazaar* called "Born 1930: The Unlost Generation." In it, she identifies the hipster as "the only extreme nonconformist of his generation" and that's not a compliment; her portrait is pretty damning. Here:

> "He is rarely an artist, almost never a writer. He may earn his living as a petty criminal, a hobo, a carnival

roustabout or a free-lance moving man in Greenwich Village."

Bird's essay inspired Norman Mailer to write his own take on the subject, ""The White Negro: Superficial Reflections on the Hipster," later that same year.

His vision of hip? It's a black thing and a jazz thing and the result of the existential reality of living under the threat of nuclear annihilation. Or as Mailer says, "It is no accident that the source of Hip is the Negro for he has been living on the margin between totalitarianism and democracy for two centuries."

The birth of the hipster, per Mailer, was the result of the (presumably white) bohemian and the (white) juvenile delinquent coming face-to-face with the Negro, and—boom!—the hipster was a fact in American life.

Mailer's essay, like the man himself, is wild and erratic. He asserts hipsters, taking their cue from suppressed African-Americans, are into the pleasures of the body more than the pleasures of the mind. He spends a lot of time dwelling on psychology and asserting that hipsters are philosophical psychopaths. He also discusses hipster lingo. And if you can suppress laughter from hearing clichéd beatnik phrases—go, make it, with it, square, swing, goof—being explained, he makes some compelling points about new language being a harbinger of new philosophy. He also talks about Marxism at the end. But frankly, I don't want to wrestle with this section, because at that point the original Stormin' Norman loses me.

Sixty years after this essay, hipster is a phrase my own kids use with scorn. To them, and I think to many others, hipsters are people who lack authenticity, they latch on to trends, their tastes are not arrived at in a natural way. When I tell them they probably would have considered me a hipster once, they say, "No, Dad. You were hip." I'm honored, of course. But obviously the definition fluctuates—a clear case of being in the eye of the beholder.

But to me, a hipster sought what was hip.

And being hip meant discovering what was cool and new before everybody else started to consume and identify with whatever the new, cool thing was. DJ Alan Freed was in the know. He had the records and the forum to present what he deemed—and listeners accepted—as hip. And by sharing that, he gets my vote for the father of modern musical hype.

While hype, as a rule, is bullshit, there are exceptions.

There are times when a critical mass of hip is reached; the world becomes ready for an organic crescendo of hype—the overflowing wave of excitement generated by the hip. In other words, the Beatles, James Brown, Zeppelin, punk rock, Run-DMC, Nirvana, Metallica, Radiohead. And so, manipulated by profiteers—promoters, producers, record labels, the band itself—hype begins.

In these instances, hype can feel authentic and organic rather than manufactured. Hip music can provoke sincere responses of excitement. This is why Public Enemy's wise counsel—don't believe the hype—isn't always on the mark; sometimes the hype is true.

Sadly, it is getting harder to discern quality from bullshit because we have recently entered a new era. Fake news has existed probably as long as language itself. That is what some humans do at times—embellish, fabricate, lie. And certainly what con men do. In 2016, of course, fake news exploded around the U.S. presidential election. There were numerous sources for this bullshit—including alt-right political actors and Russian-sponsored disinformation campaigns—but it flourished because we now have the tools to spread bullshit, namely, the Web, social media apps, and cable TV. Thanks, or no thanks, to these media platforms, we have now reached the apotheosis of manufactured hype. And this poses a problem for rationalists and realists who would like at least a few finite truths to exist. But it is also a problem for music. To understand why it's a problem a little history is in order.

Until the 20th century, the number of channels for disseminating music has been very limited. Going way back, there was the oral tradition—people learning songs from each other. Early literate societies, such as the Greeks, had musical notation, as well as papyrus, vellum, and marble, but writing music down wasn't particularly easy or common. Then there was religion, which created a culture of believers teaching other believers songs. Around A.D. 600 the forerunner of modern musical notation began. With or without notation, though, there was the tutorial, which involved musician craftsmen teaching students music. These methods are still in effect.

But in the 15th century, with the arrival of Gutenberg's moveable type printing press, the mass distribution of music via paper became a possibility. By the early 19th century, printed sheet music was popular on both sides of the Atlantic. In 1811, piano maker Samuel Chappell branched into selling sheet music, a business that blossomed and still exists today as music publishing behemoth Warner Chappell. When parlor music—the folk and popular songs of the day sung in upper- and middle-class living rooms—became the karaoke of its time in the 1800s, the hyping and selling of sheet music began in earnest. By the early 1900s sheet music was for sale in five-and-dime stores across America. Salesmen crisscrossed the country hawking songs that were hits on Broadway. I don't know if there was payola back in the day. But it's a safe bet there was some form of retail rebate for prime placement—similar to what big chain stores now call cooperative advertising—that gave stores or salespeople higher commissions (or maybe just free drinks at the bar next door) to promote one new song over another.

When radio launched, sheet music became even hotter—because more people could hear more music, coast to coast. Sheet music was the closest thing to on-demand replication of its time. If you had the music and a piano, you could play it.

Thanks to Thomas Edison and the advent of the record player, sheet music was slowly relegated to the land of musicians and their students. It remains a great way to share music. But recorded music, in tandem with the radio, rewrote the laws of hype.

With the explosion of radio, music became available almost everywhere at all times—in your home, in your car or on a hand-held portable device. And so radio became the prime driver of sales. Eventually the godfather of hype himself, Alan Freed, was busted for payola—illegal pay-to-play schemes—and died drunk, broke, and destroyed just a few years later. But with shrewdly manipulated marketing budgets and ticket giveaways, payola never really went away, and record companies easily worked around laws meant to stop it.

And then on August 1, 1981, MTV launched—and an entirely new and intensely powerful channel for hype was born. A year later, the groundbreaking digital format of CDs was introduced. Actually, groundbreaking is the wrong word.

Cataclysmic is a better choice, because the CD eventually knocked the music business's distribution channels right out from under it.

No doubt, record company bigwigs must have thought they were geniuses for creating the CD, and selling fans the same album they already owned on a new format that offered a "cleaner" sound and "bonus tracks." But by digitizing the songs, they unwittingly made their property too easy to distribute.

The rest you know: the internet, Napster, the ability to burn CDs, the easy creation of MP3s, filesharing BitTorrent, YouTube, and, most recently, subscription services. All offering seemingly every song under the sun.

What does this do to hype? Most of the old channels of distribution still exist: the oral tradition, the academic tradition, the religious tradition, sheet music, radio, records and CDs, music video, file sharing, and subscription. Plus there are new channels for distribution or at least discovery: Facebook, Twitter, Bandcamp, and Soundcloud.

But it is both too much and too damn little.

While all these channels are great in theory, mass distribution at a certain point dilutes hype. If there are too many channels to flood, if the audience is too fragmented, if SoundCloud is doing one thing, while Bandcamp is doing another and Amazon is hawking band X while Netflix is showing band Z, and Hit Radio is pumping bands D, J and W, and Pitchfork is calling indie rocker M the second coming, then the hype that built rock 'n' roll is set to crumble, because the cacophony of buzz cancels itself out.

Meanwhile, the franchises that were among the most powerful music taste makers in the previous century—Top

40 radio, MTV, prime-time TV shows—have seen their audience decline sharply.

I can hear you saying no way—just like there is hip music, there is hip media. There are Trusted Voices. And, yes, there are—your friends, music critics, Spotify, and Pandora algorithms that bunch similar genres of music together. But there are untrustworthy sources, too—social media "superstars" such as the Kardashians, Selena Gomez, and Ariana Grande, who reportedly make millions of dollars posting on Instagram. These are modern tastemakers.

And the critics you like? Bless 'em, one and all, but you probably can't totally trust them either. The attention major media outlets like *The New York Times*, the Associated Press, *Entertainment Weekly,* or *Rolling Stone* give to the arts—music, movies, and books—is dictated largely by sales, by publicists whispering hot breathy hype. By fame! By perceived heat, which isn't always based on what is hip and good, but on what is hyped and hot—which is so often dictated by record companies, movie studios, and publishers . And that's not major media's fault; it's the fucked up State of Things. The media need ad sales and page views, so writing about a Miley Cyrus concert or Stephen King's new book is more important than writing about some obscure band from say, Angola, New York or Lawrence, Kansas. Why? Because obscurity is the enemy of hype to megarich music companies.

As hype becomes more targeted, as people become more siloed in our apps, in our websites, in our echo chambers, the power of hip is being diluted, drowned out by hype, which is now social marketing driven by data and user metrics so that ads and links and videos and posts are placed in specific places and shown to specific users.

One of the scary things about this kind of targeted hype is that the critic is sidestepped. There is no need for trusted voices or insightful analysis. The hype man is everywhere—pitching bad music, crappy TV series, worthless miracle diets, conspiracy theories, or moronic political statements. It's a case of barkers on parade, winging praise, tweeting bullshit, posting, selling, hyping.

Perhaps such fragmented hype will divide itself out of existence. By parsing and tailoring and segmenting and personalizing everything, maybe the return on investment will be too small. Seriously, what if targeting foodie men who like surf music and rockabilly doesn't actually result in a sale or any "engagement"? The answer, I suppose, is some kind of return to a centralized, national conduit of music, a place where not everything is personalized and segmented but is instead lumped together in some kind of zeitgeistian, hodge-podge feed. But I can't help feeling if that's what we want, then like old school hype men Gogo and Didi, we are going to be waiting a long, long time.

# DEADHEADS AND MEKONS FANS, OR THE QUESTION OF MUSICAL CULTS

*Dear Ask a Deadhead,*

**Ann fucking Coulter? Are you kidding me?**
—Wavy Davy James, Dinkytown, Minneapolis, Minn.

*This question is so heavy, so paralyzing for so many, so soul destroying, that I'm not even going to give my man Wavy Davy a big shout-out, even though we go back to 1985 Binghamton, N.Y. There's no time for pleasantries, Wavy Davy, the community is in crisis. Never has the vibe of the Tribe been so low—at least not since the Great One went to the massive psilocybin field in the sky. This question has been weighing on many of you out there. In fact,*

*I've gotten about 714 versions of Wavy's letter, which is, as I've said, very heavy.*

*But let's unpack this very profound question and why so many are asking it. Basically it has to do with Ann fucking Coulter forcing all Deadheads to question everything we believe in and everything we love.*

*Why? Let me back up. For those of you who don't know, Ann Coulter is the worst, most hateful woman in America. And she actually gets rich being the most hateful woman in America, which makes her even worse than she is, if that's possible. She was seen on TV in 2016 getting ripped to shreds on stage during the Comedy Central* Rob Lowe Roast. *She agreed to be humiliated about her brains, personality, and horseface because she had a new book out.*

*So, to recap: Ann fucking Coulter is a horrible, nasty, mean, unrighteous, pompous, war-mongering, race-baiting, ruling-class-power-consolidating, arch-conservative, Obama-hating bitch.*

*And I'm being kind here.*

*With the appearance on Comedy Central, plus her books, plus the fact she is shamelessly stumping for Donald Trump, she's been getting a lot of press, and has pierced the consciousness of many in the Tribe. Some of you, disturbed by the notion this unspeakable hatemonger is breathing valuable air that could be used by human and animal life, researched her further and found out something truly awful.*

*Ann Coulter loves the Grateful Dead.*

*It's true. I read an interview with her. She's been to shows, man. She loves the music, but mocks the scene, which means she mocks you and mocks me and mocks the One.*

*And that is why Wavy Davy and so many of you have written.*

*Amy from Montclair, N.J., asks, "How can someone so filled with hate love Jerry and the boys? Does that cheapen the band? Or us fans?"*

*Nelson the Chillum Man, in Cobleskill, N.Y., wonders: "What is my obligation, as a human and a taper, if I see her at a show? Should I trip her so she falls down those steep arena stairs? Or should I stay true to the spirit of the Tribe and just let her be?"*

*Joey C, my pal from Tucson, Ariz., rages: "Dude, this totally kills the Tribe vibe. I feel we've been booted from the Madison Square Garden of Eden. It's like a narc has walked among us. Like the devil pissed in my bong. Like someone demagnetized my tapes. How can I get my mojo back?"*

*Brothers, sisters, dudes, dudettes! I feel your pain. Totally. And I have thought long and hard. I have fasted on this, I have sativa-ed and indica-ed on this issue for hours. I have studied the glorious 12-inch Rosetta Stones and TDK-120 tapes left behind for us to vibe on and learn the clues from the sonic temple of life.*

*And what I've found is we all have a serious case of the U.S. Blues. So when Ann Coulter waves her hate flag, it's is a reminder for us not to get too complacent—because bad shit can just sneak up on you, like Ann Coulter herself. Or as the One once sang: When life looks like easy street, there is danger at your door.*

*And Coulter liking the Dead, as horrible as that is, does not discredit the music we love. It does not discredit us. As everybody in the tribe wants to know: "Are you kind?" She is not. She is vile. The Buck Dancer would never choose her, that's for damn sure. She is an irregular, misshapen stitch in the fabric of our union. She is the single bad note in a mega-dazzling 20,000-note solo. She can listen, but she doesn't truly hear. And she may even sing along, but she's too hateful to understand the words. So people, don't push her down steps at a show, even though that is a tempting option. Better to take the high road: Light up, ignore this hideous human being—or curse her out, if you must—and remember: roll away the dew.*

HI. MY NAME IS SETH AND I AM A RECOVERING DEADHEAD.

I've been in recovery for decades, and I'm sure, after I say what needs to be said, many will think I'm cured or have morphed into a self-hating Deadhead. They might be right, too.

I can remember when that initial Dead spell was cast—my brother sent my still-in-high-school self some bootlegs and I was lured by the playful intro to "China Cat Sunflower" and the clarion call of Jerry Garcia's hookiest, most rockingest moment—that blistering seven note riff exactly 2 minutes and 18 seconds into "St. Stephen." As the only kid in school with these tunes—I'm sure it's hard for young'uns to understand, but before YouTube and Spotify, physically *owning* music was a form of status and power—I felt, at the time, I had a musical awareness and sophistication far more enlightened and adventurous than my non-Deadhead friends. And that made me cool, at least in my own twisted and arrogant head.

But eventually I fell out of love.

It was a gradual breakup. First, there was the painful realization at my maiden Dead show that the band was actually kind of boring live. With the possible exception of Bob Weir, the Dead had zero stage presence and charisma. And the slower songs put me to sleep. Maybe I just wasn't in the right frame of mind. But hell, I'd done things the righteous way: Road-tripped from upstate New York all the way to Maryland, hooked up with my German pal Thomas from high school, got high, went to the show. Ninety minutes in, I was having a what-the-fuck moment, asking, "Why am I bored?"

I went back to college. I was listening to James Blood Ulmer, Grandmaster Flash, Talking Heads, Kid Creole and the Coconuts, the Jam and the Clash, disco, reggae, King Sunny Ade, and Fela. *Everything* had more energy than the Dead to my ears. Shit, "867-5309" by Tommy Tutone had more energy and so did Madonna.

Soon, the only time I ever listened to the Dead was when I found myself getting high with Deadhead friends. And honestly, the concert tapes, with the noodling scales, the flanged bass, Jerry's high-toned, dry, meandering guitar solos, the chaotic drumming, the not very good singing—and by not very good, I mean the folksy delivery that so often failed to transcend the weak tone, the unsteady voice, the lack of dynamics—began to bug me.

I may have worn blousy shirts and had longish hair—the look of a believer—but I was definitely falling away from the tribe.

About three years after that Maryland show, the Dead played Binghamton, N.Y., where I was at school. I went to the show and once again I got bored. The meandering jams and the band's nonexistent stage presence encouraged wandering, so I walked around. I looked at the tapers, intently guarding their microphone stands, so focused on making a document that they seemed to be missing the concert itself. (Interestingly, thanks to smartphones, we are now a nation of bootleggers who choose to watch and film a live event on a tiny cell phone screen, instead of enjoying it in real time and embedding it in our memory.) I took in the hippie dancers doing their asynchronous funky skeleton moves. I wondered if the girl who had broken my heart was at the show. I didn't see her anywhere, and I was looking. After the concert, a drum circle formed outside the arena. I saw a pretty girl I knew clapping and dancing. She was in her moment, smiling, joyous; I was far away in mine. There were guys playing hacky sack, a game I thought of as completely stupid. Soccer, yes. Hacky sack? No fucking way. I felt like Scrooge McDeadhead: The whole scene struck me as vapid. I didn't want any part of it. Well, except maybe the drugs and the pretty girls.

I don't remember how, but I know I caught a ride home in the back of a complete stranger's pickup truck. Another kid got in. "Did you have a good show?" he asked me.

*Did I have a good show?* I snarled in my head, mocking the idea, because it never was *my* show—or his—to have. It was the Dead's show. They were responsible. Any problems with the show were rooted in them, and really, when the funkiest song you have in your bag is "Shakedown Street," you've got some problems.

"No, not really," I said to the Deadhead.

*Did I have a good show?*

We drove for a while. Then, at a red light, still irritated by the question, I hopped out of the pickup truck and walked the rest of the way home.

*Did I have a good show?*

Jesus.


Now, with 20/20 hindsight, I'm appalled at my hostile behavior all those years ago. The kid was just being friendly. He had good manners. He was merely articulating the caring spirit of a fellow traveler. The problem was that he didn't know his rider.

Here's the thing: Deadheads are my people. Or they should be. I'm a peace, love, and music guy. So are most Deadheads not named Ann Coulter. I grew up on folk music. So did many Deadheads. I like improvisational music. Ditto Deadheads. Many of my friends adore the Dead. And I adore my friends. But I cannot adore the Dead because of so many issues raised in previous chapters. Much of what they play doesn't suit my taste. I find the blind allegiance, the cultish single-minded focus of Deadheads absurd—an insult to all the other great music in the world. Their music often flies in the face of what I find aesthetically pleasing. Over time, what was once audacious—acid tests, improvisational jamming, not caring about bootlegged tapes—has lost its audacity. It has become—at least to me—old and stale. Add it up, and while I get what the Dead have done, and their historical importance, I find their sound, their songs, their talents overrated. So even though I lean hippie, am pro-pot and love guitar rock, folk rock, and good lyrics, I don't believe their music paves the golden road to devotion.

This isn't to say the Dead's body of work is horrible; it isn't. Their adventurous jams helped expand and define the sonic vocabulary of psychedelica. *Workingman's Dead* and *American Beauty* are acoustic gems, no question. And other albums, like the mega-trippy *Anthem of the Sun* and the darting-then-dirgy *Blues for Allah* have great moments. At their best, the band *is* an American beauty—one that blends folk, country, acid rock, jazz, trippy avant-garde jams and more into a unique sound.

But when the Dead announced they were calling it quits with a final weekend run of concerts in Chicago in the summer of 2016, the love and nostalgia for the '60s band that never had a hit record until the '80s—sadly, with the lame single "Touch of Grey"—was completely over the top. It was an unqualified love-in. And once again I began to grow disgusted with the prevailing narrative that the Grateful Dead, with or without Jerry Garcia, was just fucking awesome.

Somehow lost in the mushy nostalgia was the fact that the Dead have been one of the most erratic live bands in history. Gigs were spiked with off-key harmonies, Jerry's often cracking voice, bum notes wrecking ambitious improvised jams, that aforementioned total lack of stage presence, incessant hit-or-miss improvisations, and utterly flailing efforts to get funky—despite Phil Lesh's burbling bass and TWO drummers! Yes, the guys groove a bit, and you can hear it on "Casey Jones," "Shakedown Street," and "China Cat Sunflower," but the Grateful Dead, as innovative and expansive and groovy as they were, were often their own worst enemy.

What was the force at work that allowed the media to just clap and sing along? Was it another case of hype men gone wild?

Peace, love, and profits, maybe?

An orgy of collective nostalgia made possible by the gigantic waves of social media?

I think it's all of the above.

But there's another question that needs asking in order to understand the unconditional love-in that went down: If the Dead played a concert and there were no Deadheads in the audience, would it still be a Dead show? In other words, how much of the Dead concert experience is a result of the combustion of a cult of fans and the band they worship?

The answer, I submit, is a lot. A Dead show with no Deadheads is an oxymoronic concept. And one of the things that happens in a concert, any concert, is the unification of experience. The concert is a rite, a mass. That kid who asked me if I had a good show? That was his version of "peace be with you," and I was too dumb and rude to get it. So the nation of fans is united, on one level, by each other and by the band they have come to see.

But a commitment to tie-dye, patchouli, and spastic dancing is not a philosophy. Or maybe it is. But if it is, I'm not about to sign up because to be a member of a cult you have to believe. And I've already said the music only *sometimes* moves me—rendering me an unbeliever. Plus the rituals that make a cult a cult do not interest me. Traveling the golden road to unlimited devotion—listening to the same band over and over and over—seems more like torture than pleasure.

I have this memory of reading an article about R.E.M. In it, Michael Stipe noted the more popular the band got, the less it had in common with its fans. His point was R.E.M.'s "typical" indie rock/jangle pop, college-aged fans got waylaid as soon as "Losing My Religion" aired on MTV and exploded into a hit. Now people who probably would have never heard of them—teachers, insurance salesmen, cops, anyone, really—could sing along. Michael Stipe was grappling with being liked by people he might actually have nothing in common with. People he might not like.

That is a problem with a giant music-based cult—yes, it's a nation unified by people with the same musical taste, with people who identify with the sound, fashion, and existence. One nation under a groove, as George Clinton might put it, can be fun while you are grooving, praying, celebrating. But when the groove ends, because—sorry, Bob Weir—the music does stop, and when it does, everyone returns to their corner, just like a high school dance. And when the lights come on, you might see buzzkill Ann Coulter right beside you.

WHEN I WAS ABOUT 25 I JOINED A DIFFERENT SORT OF MUSICAL cult. Whenever the Mekons, who started out as a bunch of English punk rockers from Leeds, played in New York, I would see them. They have evolved, the Mekons, from punks who didn't really know how to play their instruments to become casual masters of country music, reggae, old English folk, and many forms of rock. Indeed the musicians who now make up the band include former Rumour drummer Steve Goulding and world music savant Lu Edmonds, who first surfaced with punk rock groundbreakers the Damned and went on to play with Kirsty MacColl and more recently with Public Image Limited. And back in the 1980s a guitarist named Dick Taylor joined the Mekons for a while. Dick may be a familiar name to some readers; he was an original member of a group called the Rolling Stones. Bill Wyman replaced him on bass and Dick went on to form the Pretty Things, a band I've mentioned elsewhere.

I like the Mekons because they have an audacious formula: rock, chaos, contempt, humor, love, and great songs. Live, they often get drunk on stage and their performances are spiked with cynicism, criticism, and comedy—in their lyrics and in their stage patter, where they discuss the world and each other.

Really, if the Grateful Dead had no stage presence, the shambolic Mekons have had it in spades. They've disrobed on stage. They've made out with each other. They've developed synchronized dances. They've talk to the audience for minutes at a time. I once saw their roadie Mitch stage-dive in his underwear. You never know what you are getting with a Mekons show, but it is almost always engaging, rocking, and usually quite charming. I like to think of them as frat rock for grad students, but that does them a great disservice by implying they are elitist smarty-pants. They are smart and arty, but the shows feel inclusive.

I liked the Mekons country-tinged albums of the mid-'80s, but I was absolutely blown away their 1989 major-label debut—which arrived some 10 years after struggling as an indie rock band, a pretty notable achievement. The album was called *Rock 'n' Roll* and began with a critique of, and a love song to, their chosen musical genre. Here are the opening lyrics to the first track on the album, "Memphis, Egypt":

> *Destroy your safe and happy lives before it is too late,*
> *the battles we fought were long and hard,*
> *just not to be consumed by rock 'n' roll*

Rock—which has "spots" before its eyes, according to a later lyric—gets compared to the devil's breath that is mistaken for "fine perfume." And that beguiling sound is irresistible; it's "something to sell your labor for" and it's "that secret where place we all want to go."

Other songs on the album attack consumer culture, drug culture, and pop culture; things, as the song "Club Mekon" states, "to be brought and sold/like rock and roll."

Many of the Mekons are now pushing 60 or have passed it. They keep writing new songs. They keep gigging, even though their audience is a tiny, tiny fraction of the Dead's. I follow them casually, not obsessively, because I find them challenging, refreshing, changing.

I say I'm a member of a "sort of" cult. That's mostly because I'm too cool for school and don't want to admit being in a cult. But also because I suspect the Mekons, as their lyrics indicate, don't trust the trappings that come with cults—the heroes, the marketing, the consumer culture that preys on the audience. They love rock 'n' roll but they are suspicious of it. And they are right to be: Weeks after A&M released *Rock 'n' Roll*, the band was dropped. Any dreams the Mekons might have had of a life made easier by the deep pockets of a major label music machine instantly vanished.

So the Mekons don't want to consume their audience, which is what cult bands do. And their fans, ironically, love them for that—and probably wouldn't mind being a little consumed.

The whole thing recalls the old Groucho Marx joke about not wanting to be in any club that would have him as member. Mekons fans, nerds who love their anti-rock rocker heroes, wouldn't want to be members of any cult devoted to a band that wanted to be a cult band. And the Mekons—who wrote a song called "Club Mekon" about seeing "a world where the dead are worshipped"—wouldn't want to be the false idols of cultish fans.

It's a very bad business model, when you think about it. But that's another reason to love 'em.

# THE COOLEST SONG YOU'VE NEVER HEARD, OR THE QUESTION OF MUSICAL ARCHEOLOGY

IN 1979, NEW WAVE VISIONARIES TALKING HEADS RELEASED *FEAR of Music*. It was the band's third album, co-produced with Brian Eno, the soundscape architect with a daunting résumé.

A member of the seminal English band Roxy Music, Eno went on to make acclaimed solo records, became the godfather of ambient music, and eventually produced a number of hugely popular albums for U2, among others.

With *Fear of Music*, Talking Heads began to expand their nerdy, nervous new wave sound. Extra layers of percussion, Eno's sonic "treatments," and added guitar tracks gave the recordings a new edge. Songs such as "Cities," "Life During Wartime," and "I Zimbra" melded the anxious, jittery delivery of Talking

Heads leader David Byrne with rhythms of African pop music. "I Zimbra" took a sound poem written by Cabaret Voltaire performer Hugo Ball in 1916 and set it to a percussion-heavy dance beat while Robert Fripp, leader of the progressive rock band King Crimson, strung wickedly sharp effects-heavy guitar solos beneath it. The novelist and Talking Heads fan Jonathan Lethem expressed the influence and impact the album had on him by writing one of the finest sentences in the history of rock criticism. It ends this way: "I might have wished to wear the album *Fear of Music* in place of my head so as to be more clearly seen by those around me."

Two years after *Fear of Music*, Byrne and Eno released an album called *My Life in the Bush of Ghosts*. It didn't sell as well as *Fear of Music*, which eventually sold half a million copies by 1985. But it became hugely influential.

If *Fear of Music* expanded the sonic template for Talking Heads, *My Life in the Bush of Ghosts* expanded it for pop music in general. The album was stuffed with new ideas, or if not new, then borrowed from avant-garde sources, such as music concrete and experimental film soundtracks. The result was a collage-like work that is a forerunner of the mashup. Working with found sounds—samples of other singers, radio ranters, and even an exorcist—Eno and Byrne mixed these vocal elements over dance beats, providing a vision that influenced a huge swath of songwriters, DJs, and producers. Public Enemy sound guru Hank Shocklee, for example, credits the album with helping shape '80s hip-hop. The album expanded the unofficial and unwritten rules of pop music by demonstrating how found sounds, interviews, and other musical recordings could be used in the mixing of a pop song.

In 1977, two years before the release of *Fear of Music*, a fledgling band in Nairobi, Kenya, released a single. The band was called Makonde, which is the name of an East African tribe famous for its distinctive wood cut sculptures. The single was called "Soseme Makonde." Unless you were in Kenya in 1977, the chance you've ever heard this song is minuscule. But I offer it up as a Rosetta Stone of alternative music and, yes, modern dance music.

"Soseme Makonde" was released in Kenya on Makonde's first and only album, *Matata Riots*. The single got a lot of airplay on the Voice of Kenya, which is how I heard it as a 13-year-old (my family had relocated there from New York because of my father's job). And I even remember reading about the band at the time in the country's two English-language papers, *The Nation* and *The Standard*. A "Soseme Makonde" single was also released in France in 1977. I have no proof Brian Eno or David Byrne ever heard it. But I'm betting, somehow, some way, they did, because so much of what showed up on *Fear of Music* and *My Life in the Bush of Ghosts* was foreshadowed by this obscure track from a flash-in-the-pan band from Kenya.

After years of sporadic internet searches, I finally found "Soseme Makonde" posted on YouTube by a Polish disco fan in 2016. The song was even better than I remembered. It opens with murmuring, mumbling, muttering voices, instantly catching your attention the same way another 1977 release did—Marvin Gaye's "Got to Give It Up (Pt. 1)"—except Gaye's song captured the laidback sounds of people at a party while the guys on "Soseme" sound like, well, zombies. Then the song launches into a fierce, galloping percussion groove and, slowly, a busy, Afro-disco bass line fades in. The groove is very similar to the one driving "I

Zimbra." In fact, the lyrics of "I Zimbra" scan very easily against the music of "Soseme Makonde."[7] Then calm, cool singing starts—with the chorus. It's a cross between a unison chant and a hymn.

This singing is interesting for a number of reasons. The leader of Makonde was a Tanzanian-born Greek national named Taso Stephanou. The word "soseme" is not a Swahili word. But the rest of the song is in Swahili. But "soseme" means "save me" in Greek. So the song's main lyric seems to translate as "Save me, save me, Makonde." Releasing a disco-Afro-funk hybrid Swahili song in Kenya and France based on a Greek word by a band named after a Tanzanian tribe seems pretty odd. But it's the sound that matters to listeners, especially with dance music.[8]

Not that "Soseme Makonde" doesn't hold its own lyrically. It does. Here's a rough translation of some lines:

> *Yeah, mother, I had your music*
> *Yeah, father, we will sing your song*
> *But everything is wind*
>
> *There is no music in our place*
> *But everything is wind*
> *In your head*

---

7   In fairness to Byrne and Eno, the mashup has proven that almost any lyric can "scan" against any other piece of music. But some words scan more easily and gracefully than others. This is one of those cases.

8   There is no Dylan of disco, because the groove and the hook are the prime movers of the music. With dim mantras like "Born to Be Alive" and "Dance, Dance, Dance (Yowsah, Yowsah, Yowsah)," much of the poetry is in the motion of the music and dancers.

Those chanting vocals I was talking about? They have an echo-y reverb that make it sound like a forerunner of new age/disco/chant, a solemn genre popularized by projects like the German new age dance act Enigma and turned into million sellers in the early 1990s.

As the song rushes forward, that calm chorus develops: "Ma–ah–ah–ah–ah–ah Makonde!" And then, after verses in Swahili start, something really cool happens—a burbling electro-break cuts in.

In 1977.

On a Kenyan record.

Made in a Kenyan recording studio.

It lasts two measures after every line of verse, and it resembles the synthetic disco sounds of Giorgio Moroder's rumbling keyboard figures in Donna Summer's proto-techno "I Feel Love," also released in 1977. The more I listen to it, the section feels like someone is hammering two echo-drenched notes on a mini-Moog. But, really, I don't know what the hell it is. Still, this modern, robotic touch breaks in repeatedly after each verse. And then, here come the humans—the singers all screeching and whooping in a different break. The kind of wacky, out-of-context sounds that fill *My Life in the Bush of Ghosts*. And yes, some of the whoops sound like a certain New York band that formed in Rhode Island.

Then it's back to that holy-sounding, somber chant. And by now, when I hear it, it sounds less like Enigma and more like a forerunner of the long, drawn-out phrases that appear a few years later on the song "Born Under Punches" from Talking Heads' groundbreaking 1980 album *Remain in Light*. But maybe I'm projecting.

As the final "Makonde" is sung—the kick drum thumping its unwitting acid house best—the electro-break sneaks in for the last measures. And then it's over.

The coolest song you've never heard.*[9]

Why am I writing about it? Why is it important to me? Because it's a missing link! A song that possibly influenced two of pop music's most important visionaries, that helped translate pop music ideas from Africa into Western pop. Everyone knows Eno and David Byrne were soaking up African music. Hell, they were probably doing it years before Paul Simon even knew what Soweto was. But this? From Kenya? You have to understand: Kenya, a tourist paradise in the 1970s, is a country that gets little respect in the international African pop music derby dominated over many decades by Nigeria with Fela Kuti's Afrobeat and King Sunny Ade's juju, Zaire and the mind-bending dance-o-phonic soukous of Franco and Tabu Ley Rochereau, the proto-blues of Mali (Ali Farka Touré, scores of griots, and, lately, Tinariwen), and the choral and township jive sounds of South Africa (Ladysmith Black Mambazo, Mahlathini and the Mohotella Queens). So the idea that a strange, totally obscure band—they didn't even play benga, Kenya's brand of pop—could be such an influence and actually inspired the template for unabashed geniuses like David Byrne or Brian Eno—well, this is big stuff.

This, in fact, is a miracle. Like finding undiscovered musical DNA. The ideas didn't just spring forth from Eno and Byrne's impressive brains. They were influenced. Just as the title for *My*

---

9   You can hear it. Go to YouTube and search Soseme Makonde. A saint named OssesTheDiscoKing who lives in Poland found this song and posted it. You can also find the B side of the single on YouTube. It's called "Manzara."

*Life in the Bush of Ghosts* was taken from a much-lauded novel of the same name by Nigerian writer Amos Tutuola, some of the musical and vocal ideas—the beats and rhythms and studio mixes—were taken from not only Afrobeat and the avant-garde, but from, yes, Makonde!

Byrne and Eno are not alone. Everyone borrows. Everyone builds on what came before in artistic pursuits. Influences are great things, but there is an invisible line between being influenced and being saturated by an influence. When a singer or a band makes music that sounds very obviously like something that came before, it is not usually perceived as a good thing. There are all kinds of reasons for this.

For one, it smacks of being unoriginal or derivative, or inauthentic. Having a unique, singular sound creates a musical identity. Artists have styles, tones, timbres, voices. It's a strange thing in the music business that stylistic replication is rewarded—think of all the musical movements and how they are related. From new wave to grunge, from Motown to hair metal, from punk to disco, the music within a genre will have traits in common. And that commonality is considered a good thing, until it becomes too common that it borders on cliché. Then it becomes a musical rehash, a knockoff.

This is why tracking and gauging new influences, unlikely influences, is an interesting thing. *Fear of Music* and *Bush of Ghosts* were influenced by many things. And they in turn influenced a ton of other bands. White rock bands became frighteningly proficient in funk-filtered pop. Duran Duran, A Certain Ratio, PigBag, and !!! were all influenced by the groundbreaking sounds of *Fear of Music* and *Bush of Ghosts*. They may never cop to it, but even established stars, like Peter Gabriel, David Bowie, and Paul

Simon, took notice of new grooves, expanded instrumentation, and created their own danceable work.

Theft and inspiration and sourcing have deep roots. Some of our most successful and influential bands have pilfered the past. Led Zeppelin has riled more than one blues purist for harvesting sonic wonders from the likes of John Lee Hooker and spinning them into rock 'n' roll gold. The Isley Brothers have accused the Beatles of ripping them off—using "Twist and Shout" and other tunes to build their fame.

Listen, it's entirely possible I'm wrong. Despite the striking similarities, I would say it's 99 percent PROBABLE that Eno and Byrne NEVER heard "Soseme Makonde."

Parallel universes DO exist. Take the book you are reading right now. I came up with the title for this book by cracking a joke during a thread discussing air guitar on Facebook. I offered some cockamamie theory and said, "You can read about in my book, Metaphysical Graffiti." I was so proud of that joke, I wrote a whole book. But when I met with my old pal and book cover designer Kevin, he said, "*Metaphysical Graffiti*? That's an album by the Dead Milkmen, right?"

My jaw dropped. I'd never heard of this album. I've never heard a single Dead Milkmen song other than "Bitchin' Camaro." I couldn't believe that my title wasn't totally original. Not only that, but I couldn't believe this was happening to me again! One year earlier, I wrote a novel called *Nuns with Guns*. I was so confident this was such a great, original title, I didn't bother searching for any rivals. Then my friend Gary read the novel. He said, "You know there's a B-movie called *Nuns with Big Guns*?"

So accidents will happen. Something that seems like clear-cut appropriation may not be. I have written two books now—TWO—with titles I thought were original, but weren't.

But back to Byrne and Eno and my theory.

Byrne loves obscurities from far-flung places, as he has repeatedly proven with his excellent Luaka Bop record label. And Makonde was reportedly signed to EMI and toured Europe—with Manu Dibango and English reggae band Aswad—where Eno might have seen them. Meanwhile, Taso Stephanou is also said to have gone to the U.S. to set up a tour that, apparently, never happened. I have no idea where he went. But New York seems like a reasonable destination. So anything is possible—it's hardly a stretch that a Greek-Swahili lyrical mashup could easily inspire the genius of "I Zimbra."

I'm sure some people will say, who cares? But music evolves. It is based on innovation, on understanding what came before. That's why digging for musical breakthroughs and milestones is important. Sonic archeology can help us understand old works and build new ones. That is one of the reasons why people *study* music. So even if Eno and Byrne swear on a stack of Robert Rauschenberg-signed copies of Talking Heads' *Speaking in Tongues* that they never heard "Soseme Makonde," it doesn't matter. The ideas of Makonde, the work of Makonde, are proof of a new sound at a new time in a new place. How Taso Stephanou—who reportedly became a music promoter in South Africa—and his bandmates got to it is anybody's guess. But they did. And don't take my word for it. You can go listen on YouTube now and hear music history in the making—all by yourself.

It's almost enough to make me love the Internet.

# TO COVER OR TO RUN FOR COVER? OR THE QUESTION OF SONIC FORGERY

HERE'S A STORY THAT SETS UP ONE OF THE MOST PERPLEXING questions in rock. What defines a good cover song and why do people love them so much when so many of them are completely unoriginal, safe, and boring?

## IN MY "GLEE" TRIBUTE TO LOU REED EPISODE

*In* My "Glee" Tribute to Lou Reed Episode, *I'm the new kid everyone is talking about in school because I used to be in a successful* boy band, but I quit after seeing a photo of Justin Timberlake wearing his hair in cornrows.

So everyone is wondering if I'm going to join the New Directions glee club and why the heck I'm living in Lima, Ohio. But I'm that tall, really good-looking, silent type, so I'm not saying anything.

I'm in the school cafeteria when Tina Cohen-Chang says, "Hey, Jon, I hear you're a great singer. Are you going to join New Directions?"

I shake my head no.

"Why not? We're great!"

I shrug. I really don't want to go there.

"That's not an answer. Have you heard us?"

"Of course I have. Look, you guys have had gay kids, a kid in a wheelchair, and you even had a quarterback, but where is your alterna-misfit like me, who hates half the music you sing? How am I gonna fit in?"

"It's so easy to be a hater, Jon. What do you think we should be doing?"

And then, on the soundtrack, these two bass notes glissando from G to C and then slide back again. You know the song. Everyone does. And I say, "Holly came from Miami, F-L-A…"

So I lead a killer version of Lou Reed's drag-queen classic "Walk on the Wild Side," mincing down the food line, turning myself into one of his characters, tonging a heap of spaghetti over my head, holding cantaloupes to my chest, and applying ketchup for lipstick. I even cue the food-service workers: "And all the colored girls go, 'Doo do doo do doo doo di doo do doo do doo do di doo.'" Then Mercedes and Santana, who are visiting because it's alumni day, join in. The whole cafeteria cheers when we finish.

*I go to the bathroom in* My "Glee" Tribute to Lou Reed Episode, *so I can wash off the ketchup and get the spaghetti out of my hair, and Tina comes in to tell me how awesome I was. She says I should attend the next New Directions rehearsal and try out. Maybe I can even give them an edge. Then, because we're in the bathroom and looking at ourselves, she sings "I'll Be Your Mirror," which is a song that, like, everyone name-checks as great and sensitive. And, even though I'm tall, dark, and mysterious, my eyes get watery for a second, but I wipe them really quickly.*

*At rehearsal, the kids are all talking about me. Will I show up or not? Artie (the kid in the wheelchair), Blaine (a gay kid), and Marley (a new girl) decide to go looking for me and roam through the halls, singing "I'm Waiting for the Man" and doing cartwheels and splits, and even a wheelchair wheelie. It's so upbeat you could almost forget it's a song about scoring heroin.*

*When I finally show up, I say I'll try out on one condition.*

*"Anything!" Blaine says.*

*"I want us to sing a two-minute version of 'Metal Machine Music, Part 1.'"*

*"No! Don't do it!" It's Rachel, back from Juilliard for alumni day. "I know a former student who heard a performance of it at Columbia University and went nuts. It's pure noise."*

*"Well, that's my requirement," I say. "The club is called New Directions, right?"*

*"But the new direction isn't insanity!" says Rachel, who has had a really hard time this year. "Listen, you guys, I love you all. But don't do it. It's like a … a descent into madness."*

*Rachel is tearful and pleading. And I feel a little like a jerk in* My "Glee" Tribute to Lou Reed Episode, *but I say what I have to: "Art isn't always beautiful, man."*

*The principal, Sue Sylvester, who is played by the awesome Jane Lynch, storms in. "Rachel! What's wrong?" she says.*

*Artie rats me out: "He wants to sing 'Metal Machine Music.'"*

*Sue gasps in horror. "Look what you've done with your horrible, hateful music," she says to me. "Get out of here, Mister Misery Guts!"*

*I stand up. I weigh three choices. If we were off screen and out of character, I would definitely sing her "Sweet Jane." But we are in character, so I consider wooing Sue with "Pale Blue Eyes," which is my personal favorite Lou song. But then I think, Duh, this is "Glee," so I launch into "I Love You, Suzanne." It's a fabulous, finger-snapping version that makes you want to dance. The "Glee" gang loves it, and by the end even Sue is making goo-goo eyes at me.*

*"We don't have to do 'Metal Machine Music,'" I say, walking over to Rachel. "Are you okay?"*

*She smiles through her tear-stained face, and then, with that crystalline voice and the following lyrics, leads us to the finale of My "Glee" Tribute to Lou Reed Episode:*

I've been set free and I've been bound
To the memories of yesterday's clouds

*It's "I'm Set Free," the glorious, pounding, punky, gospel-tinged song that Lou Reed wrote for the Velvet Underground. Mercedes steps in for the second verse to blast it to the stratosphere, and then we're all in, singing our hearts out, the New Directions, finally going somewhere different, soaring high above the Top 40, trumpeting "I'm set free!" And we are whirling, swirling, like those kids at Phish shows, except we actually know how to dance. It is so good, so moving, it doesn't matter that the last line is a bit cynical: "I'm set free to find a new illusion."*

## METAPHYSICAL GRAFFITI

*"Are you in, Jon?" asks Brittany, who is back from M.I.T. for alumni day at the very end of* My "Glee" Tribute to Lou Reed Episode.

*I know she's trouble. And I know a Styx tribute show can't be too far away, either. But this is a force of nature, my new illusion. So I say the only thing I can: "Hell, yes!"*

WHEN I WAS A KID IN THE '70S, A COMPANY CALLED K-TEL RECORDS ran TV ads hawking collections of Top 40 hits played by cover bands.

This always horrified me because even in the brief snippets of the songs that aired, I could hear that this was not the original recording of, say, "The Night Chicago Died" by Paper Lace. It sounded slightly different, and therefore, to my 10-year-old mind, suckier than the original hit. I always wondered whether the people who ordered these records realized these were covers, or if they did know (hell, I was 10 and I knew) and it didn't bother them. I'm guessing many of the sales were made to adults with credit cards who were buying them for their kids and grandkids. But I have no way of knowing if this is true.

My problem then was that the songs, the covers, didn't sound like the originals, and the advertisers were trying to trick music fans into buying something fake.

The art world has a name for these types of clones—forgeries. A forgery can be lauded for technical brilliance, but it's a word largely without positive connotations. For example, I'm betting very few people have ever sought out forgeries of Van Gogh's "Starry Night" because the copies add something new the original lacks.

Speaking of the art world, there is a tradition of mimicry as artists strive to match the techniques of masters. But, as far as I know, Monet never "covered" Manet and then displayed it in a show.

Pop art and conceptual art have broadened the playful and exploratory world of visual covers—art commenting on previous works. But in the world of music, reproducing songs doesn't have much of a stigma one way or the other for most people. Partly that's because music is written to be performed, and classical music is precisely notated so it can be performed. Rare is the artist who writes down the oils or brushes used in the making of a painting so it can be reproduced.

Ironically, now my problem with covers is—usually—they never sound different enough.

And yet decades later, with the enormous success of shows like *Glee* and *American Idol*, it appears few people share my scorn of the cover song.

I find this incredibly distressing.

In a sense, I've already touched on why people love cover songs while discussing taste and why, or rather how, anyone could possibly like Rush. The brain likes the familiar. Musical taste is socialized. We like the sounds we know.

So part of the success of a TV show like *Glee* was that it regurgitated the familiar, and part of the success of *American Idol* was that judges and audiences encouraged vocal counterfeiting and rewarded the familiar. Originality—new songs, new arrangements, new sounds, and even new looks—was rarely encouraged.

There were no punk rock episodes on *Glee* filled with Joy Division or Black Flag songs. There was no tribute to Nick Drake or Muddy Waters. The songs were almost exclusively Top 40, which makes sense if you are trying to be a popular show. And in my limited viewing of the series, the arrangements hewed pretty close to the original tunes, embellished, as you might expect, with some glee-club vocal-flourishes.

The success of *Glee*—and the jukebox musicals that fill Broadway theaters, faithfully regurgitate the songbooks of Carole King, the Beatles and the Four Seasons—all speak to the easy power of the straight-forward cover song.

I say straight-forward cover, because a good cover—an *original* cover, oxymoron that it is—is hard to find.

The easy cover, a straightforward rendition of a song that has already been written—a musical forgery—is generally harmless, unless it's a bad song to begin with, or it clogs the airwaves. That said, rethinking a cover, taking an old song and trying to improve it, reinterpret it, rearrange it, put a new spin on it, is a far more interesting and appealing thing.

I realize many musicians just want to play the great music that has gone before them. Of course they do. But as a listener, what do I care? I can instantly listen to the original recording, especially in the world of Spotify and other subscription services.

Here are the standard reasons to perform a straight cover of a song:

- Fill out a set
- Give a new audience something familiar
- Pay tribute to masters
- It's fun to play a great song
- Profit by it in some way

These are all honorable motivations. Here, however, are reasons not to perform straight covers:

- If the original is a great song, chances are you will not improve on it
- The cover will never have the "aura" of the original[10]
- If you don't improve on it, you show a lack of interpretive skill
- If you don't improve on it, you will bore the audience, which is just lame

Some people—like the "pros" that judge TV talent shows and the unthinking audiences that salivate over so many reality show performances—think faithfully duplicating a song is the definition of a good cover.

And while that is a definition, it is completely wrong.

The best covers recontextualize, rethink, rearrange a song. They give you something new to think about and redefine the song. A great cover makes you wonder, which version is the definitive version for you. It could be something as simple as a striking interpretation: Run-DMC's rap/rock version of Aerosmith's "Walk This Way"; a striking juxtaposition: New wavers Talking Heads tackling Al Green's "Take Me to the River";

---

10 The idea of the "aura" comes from philosopher and critic Walter Benjamin and his essay "The Work of Art in the Age of Mechanical Reproduction (or Reproducibility)." Benjamin, writing mostly about film, painting, and mechanical reproduction, claims a work of art has unique aura at the moment of creation that is lost when it goes into mass production. Benjamin didn't write about pop music in his essay, but I'm guessing he would say the rock songs we all love are missing an aura because they are mass produced copies. It's interesting to think that a live cover—a copy—might actually have *more* of an aura—or create an aura—because its performance isn't mechanized. But from my perspective, the recording is the "original work" most fans hear, so the cover will likely lose the recording's aura (which Benjamin would say doesn't exist).

Hüsker Dü blasting the Byrds' "Eight Miles High" or, one of my all-time favorite transformations, Jimi Hendrix's version of Dylan's "All Along the Watchtower."

The examples above all involve good bands covering strong original material. But a more creative cover tactic is to, as Paul McCartney might put it, take a bad song and make it better. This is where *American Idol* and *The Voice* could have shined, given the crap that so often cracks the Top 40. But recycling music in original ways is hard, and good covers are really, really hard. That's why the aforementioned covers are great: They take a good song and kick it into a higher gear.

My list of great covers would also include Amy Winehouse's version of a song called "Valerie." When I first heard it, I assumed it was a Winehouse original—a mysterious, soulful song of yearning. But I was wrong. Winehouse had landed on an interesting choice. The original "Valerie," by a Liverpool band called the Zutons, is the too-rare rock tune spiked with a horn section. It's a high-energy song in the Zutons' hands. The video interprets the lyrics with a moderately amusing story line: Valerie, if you've been wondering, has been in prison, and the Zutons go get her.

Amy's version turns a peppy, upbeat ditty about lust into a moving, bluesy, R&B-grooving song about loss and absence and lust. Both songs use the same lyrics. But the Winehouse version takes on a new layer, it recasts and reinvents the song. It takes a not bad song and makes it much better.

Amy Winehouse used to perform another popular cover at her concerts, the reggae classic "Monkey Man." Originally sung by Toots & the Maytals, many have covered the song. Amy—it feels wrong calling the intimate singer by her last name—amps up the great tune with a crack band. They have fun with it, fooling with the tempo, the feel, but remaining totally true to the song. It's a delight. But it is not nearly as interesting as the yearning, bluesy pathos of "Valerie."

The curse of the cover becomes more apparent when Hollywood gets involved. Efforts to turn *Sgt. Pepper's Lonely Hearts Club Band* and *Tommy* into movies with new soundtracks toyed with reinvention. But the directors and music supervisors of those projects were in a tough spot: Change too much, and you are messing with perfection. Change too little, and what's so special about the soundtrack?

Almost none of the movie version songs come close to the originals. In fact, only "Got to Get You Into My Life," Paul McCartney's Motown-influenced, horn-charged love song to pot from *Revolver*, gets a truly worthy overhaul. The band that pumps it full of new life, Earth Wind & Fire, is a Chicago-born group with serious chops and great singers. EWF's version brings more of everything—harmony, brass, sass, beat—than the original. It is a transformed song. It feels fresh, remade. It is different, and therefore has a reason to exist! I still prefer the original to the cover, if only because the Beatles' take on Motown is so refreshing and, well, perfect.

Jazz, frequently built on an ever-evolving group of standards, is fundamentally improvisational music. Adding new elements, melodies, rhythms, and arrangements, jazz already applies the ideal rules for covers. Jazz bands take previously written material and embellish it. The centuries-old form of popular music known as classical is also built on standard repertory, but its performances are largely static. Orchestras play and re-play composers' work faithfully. This makes sense on a number of levels. Functionally, reworking a symphonic score—and assembling a symphony to play it—is a complex undertaking. Aesthetically, too, the power of Beethoven and the beauty of, say, Bach, don't seem worthy of altering. Really, who the hell is going to one-up Bach? It's kind of like covering the Beatles—the chances of improving on the original are slim to none.

Folk music is intrinsically static. It is old, *traditional* music. But it too evolves and mutates, like a generational game of telephone. What was sung 100 years ago morphs as it is passed from singer to singer. Forms like the blues and bluegrass have room for improvisation and change.

For centuries, folk music was the pop—as in popular—music of its time. And as interest in folk once again wanes, pop music has become the music the folk now listen to. We sing pop songs—cover them faithfully—because they are familiar and comforting in a world that moves faster than ever before and cuts ties to the past faster than ever before. And so I should be more forgiving of pop covers. And sometimes I am. Really.

Ironically, when I was in a rock band, back when dinosaurs roamed the earth, we played our own songs and a few radically reworked covers (a ska verison of Bad Company's "Can't Get Enough of Your Love"; a version of T. Rex's "Mambo Sun" with Afro-pop guitar breaks), and I can remember telling friends, "If I ever play in a cover band, please kill me."

This was a stupid attitude for many reasons, I realize now. What opened my eyes (or ears) to the level of stupidity, I'm embarrassed to say, were wedding bands. Sometimes, when I haven't gigged in ages, I think, man, maybe it would be fun to play in a wedding band. Everyone at the gig is happy. Everyone is hopeful. Everyone is nostalgic. Everyone dances. The musicians actually get paid. And some bands just kick it.

At a wedding, dancing is usually the thing. You don't have to worry about writing worthy lyrics, as you would in your own band. The bride and groom and their guests having a good time is the only thing that matters. Music helps facilitate this. Remember the wisdom of so many kids on *American Bandstand*? They explained what makes a song work: "It's got a good beat and you can dance to it." That's pretty much all you need as a wedding band.

Long story short: I'm a hypocrite. Here I am, railing about cover bands, and yet part of me would love to play in one now (a funky one, with a horn section). Not only that, but I have been to see a Beatles tribute band on Broadway. It was like going to church. When the Beatle clones played "Hey Jude," the entire audience stood up, swayed and sang out the hymn: "Na, na, na-na-nananana nanananan hey Jude." I loved it more than I ever expected to.

So what does this mean? I dunno. It probably means I should qualify what I've been saying. I guess, if you are going to do a straight cover, do it well. Either figure out how to duplicate the "aura"—like *Beatlemania* or some other obsessive tribute band—or pick up on the forces that made you want to cover a song in the first place: its musical authenticity, creativity, and originality, and add your own.

The cover conundrum is not just about musicians; it's about listeners, too. If hearing a flimsy facsimile of a song floats your boat, who am I to argue? But if music is a nourishing force, we should be listening better and demanding better. At the risk of stating the obvious, understanding the construction and inner workings of anything—cars, movies, poems, furniture, food—helps you evaluate it. That doesn't mean everyone needs to take a music theory class, although I wish I had. It just means listening to and thinking about the piece and asking questions: Do I like it? Why? What am I responding to? Why?

So when Jimi Hendrix reworks Bob Dylan's "All Along the Watchtower" and injects his vocal delivery with a sense of desperation and then paints the anxiety in a soundscape of ominous guitar sounds and a blistering, effects-heavy solo, he hasn't just covered the song—which he absolutely has—he's transcended Dylan's original version and created his own new song. Not every musician is a Hendrix or an Amy Winehouse, obviously; these are the rare breeds. But what they do with other people's material is what musicians should all aspire to do: Create music that reinterprets, pays tribute, and awakens, that extends melodies and embellishes beats.

And you know what? When someone gets it right, like Amy did with "Valerie," you might even cover that cover in a wedding band. It'll be great. But hey, add something to it—a cowbell, say. It almost always works.

# CAN A DJ SAVE YOUR LIFE? OR THE OXYMORONIC QUESTION OF EDM CONCERTS

*DJ Philosophy 101*
*Dr. DJ MC² 3-4:30 p.m., Tue-Thu, Rm 210, Baxter Hall*

This survey course probes the major philosophical questions confronting all DJs—from the eternal enigma of when one can truly be considered to have gotten the party started, to the perplexing issues surrounding the search for the perfect beat, including Fredric Von Barking's mind-numbing trope, "When searching for the perfect beat, how can we know it if we have never heard it before?"

The class will begin with a survey of the evolution of the DJ from the charismatic, radio-driven hype-masters of the '50s and '60s, to the hairy-chested, mustachioed mega-mix disco gods of the

'70s, to rap-happy wheels of steel cut creators of the '80s and '90s, and finally, to today's incredibly lazy laptop-wielding, social media-banging plagiarists.

Once the historical and sociological introductions are covered, the bulk of the class will probe the questions asked by the great DJ philosophers. We'll examine Rene "Boom-Boom" LeFay's exploration into whether great songs like "Uptown Funk" and "Good Times" can subvert free will; Soren Johansen's quest to quantify the importance of a DJ's personal party anthem; and Pierre Fantastique's classic DJ trope: if you rocked the house at 4:27 a.m. on a Tuesday but the dance floor was empty, did you make a sound?

Work requirements:

1. There will be a mid-term made of short answer questions. Sample questions:
   - Is the meaning of life to:
     - a. Get your freak on?
     - b. Rock the party?
     - c. Pump up the jams?

     Explain your answer.
   - Which disco classic is more existential: "Born to Be Alive" or "Got to Be Real"? Why?
   - Can a perfect beats-per-minute ratio exist? If so, what is it and why is it perfect?
   - If a modern production of The Iliad were to replace the Trojans and the Greeks with two warring DJ nations, should Skrillex or Steve Aoki play Odysseus? Discuss.

2. *Students in Week 8 will rock the mic and present their own 60-second personal party anthem and grade each other.*
3. *Final paper. Students will choose one of three questions and write a 10-page paper. Here are last year's questions:*
   - *Explain why French DJs are so good, given that French pop music had previously been a black hole for decades. C'est impossible, n'est pas?*
   - *KC and the Sunshine Band or Daft Punk? Discuss.*
   - *If a DJ were to mash up a number of mashups into a new mashup, would such radical decontextualization impede the house-rocking qualities of the source material the DJ has mashed by fragmenting and stripping the sonic points of reference that help make mashups cool? In other words, would that suck?*

*Syllabus*: *Rhythmic Complexities of House* by Thomas, Vickers & Lopez; *The Delirium of Crowds* by Soren Johansen; *I Spin Therefore I Am* by Rene LeFay; *Being and Then Getting Totally High* by Pierre Fantastique; *Le Freak: A Study of the Physiological Impact of Nile Rodgers' Guitar on Ravers in Ibiza* by Dr. Bobbi Bonanno.

HERE'S AN IMAGE:

A man or woman stands on a stage or DJ booth holding one half of a pair of a headphones over one ear. The DJ takes his or her free hand, turns it into a fist, and pumps it in time to a thundering 4/4 beat. Fans and dancers pump their fists back at the DJ, cheering the mixmaster and his (or her) sounds, which are very often prerecorded or preprogrammed or both. Lasers blast, flash, and swirl, spotlights roam over the crowd, video images fill huge overhead screens. The DJ grabs a mic and bellows, "Make some noise!" or "Fuck yeah!" The beats pummel and amp the crowd. And the DJ—the MC, the stage general, the magician who conjures up this sensory party—is the lord of all the smiling, throbbing, drugged-up believers he or she surveys.

For music fans who remember a time when hip-hop was a fairly novel medium, or hadn't even been invented yet, and "bands" with "musicians" generally dominated the popular music landscape, this image is hard to understand.

Or accept.

That said, it has become a dominant image for younger concertgoers who dig EDM, which stands for electronic dance music.

The idea of the DJ as a musical star—as a *musician*—is not something that translates easily for many older music fans. And by older music fans, I mean me and, if you are over 45, you. True, DJs—disc jockeys—had been around for 15 years before Alan Freed roamed the airwaves. But they were adored for their on-air personality and the music they played. It wasn't until the '70s, when disco evolved to extended jams, and turntable wizardry began to wow listeners, that spinning records became more widely viewed as a *musicianly* pursuit. "Playing" a turntable, "mixing" one record together with another, was a performance. You could actually see and hear music created, especially when turntablists, as they were called, would "scratch" records, manipulating them back and forth beneath a record player needle to create new sounds. (I apologize for stating what will be obvious to many readers; others may have never seen a turntable, much less witnessed "scratching.")

Before EDM was called EDM, it was called dance music, or disco or club music. By any name, the coolness of this R&B/funk offshoot could be mesmerizing. Immaculately produced hypno-jams by Giorgio Moroder and Cerrone took the orchestral grooves honed by Barry White and turned them into synthesized disco epics. It didn't suck, unless you were a white, uptight suburbanite, threatened by a new movement that was all about movement. It never sucked. It was fun. An entire generation of DJs followed, creating subgenres. The mixer had secret powers. Back in the previous century, New York-based disco crew Indeep had a 1982 song called "Last Night a DJ Saved My Life." It is a classic mix of soul singers, chicken-scratching disco guitar, and Chic-esque cool. And I do, sometimes, still believe that yes, a DJ can maybe, somehow, save your life. Not that EDM should be confused with an EMT, but dance music and dance music culture—and here I'm thinking not just of the transcendence and joy of moving to music, but also of a more existential salvation documented, say, in the film *Paris Is Burning*, where voguing and drag balls created a sense of place and purpose for LGBT communities—can help sustain life, because that is something music does: unites and nourishes.

I don't find much of what I hear in the EDM era particularly appetizing, though. Energizing, like speed, yes. Fun like house music, sure. With the depth, artistry, and impact of the best hip-hop? Not so much. I can see how it still provides meaning and escape for fans. But EDM's life-sustaining powers are very much in doubt for me.

My problem—besides being old and crotchety and given to yelling "get off my lawn" in my sleep—involves ideas about musicianship, performance, appropriation, and nomenclature. But before I go any further, let's lay down some definitions: EDM DJs mostly play other people's music. Some of them, like Aoki and Avicii, cut token tracks of their own. EDM artists are DJs who play strictly their own music. These would include people like Skrillex, Afrojack, DeadMau5. Finally, there are electronic music artists, a wide-raging term that is not solely focused on the dance floor. Some EMAs never play live. Some are fully sequenced and trigger everything live, while some use acoustic instruments and even play them live.

Records—or CDs, for that matter—are almost never involved in "live" EDM, which makes the term EDM DJ, or "disc jockey," oxymoronic. "Instruments" have been almost completely eliminated, replaced by computers, programs and music files. In fact, a student of EDM assures me there are DJs who rely on two-hour DAT tapes to do shows and CAN'T spin records because they need to match the lighting cues at mega festivals.

This means that EDM DJs and EDM artists are both hard-pressed to deliver an actual live performance of their art form.

It also turns out EDM virtuosos don't need to actually play a single musical instrument. They require zero knowledge of pitch or keys. And since digital music-editing programs allow pitch and key manipulation, you could even make the argument that they don't actually need ears, to make sure a recording sounds okay. They just need eyes so they can see their mix on a computer screen. Rock the house!

So you get why some people consider this type of music utter bullshit, right? There's no dues-paying in EDM, compared to the callous-raising agony of learning guitar, or headache-inducing monotony of learning the drums. Even Paris Hilton can DJ. No kidding, the millionaire, reality show trustafarian, and porn tapestress bimbo is a DJ. I swear. Google her.

The idea of a star tethered to his computer doesn't work for me. Even though, if I'm honest, it should, because I don't mock classical conductors who stand before an audience leading a symphony. So why do I scoff at the image of the fist-pumping EDM DJ?

Two reasons. One, as I've said, huge amounts of the music is canned. I scorned most preprogrammed music at the beginning of the digital revolution, when samplers allowed band to create all kinds of sounds and syncopations by working them out beforehand and then triggering entire musical sequences of a song. It was nifty on a sonic level, but lame on a performance level. Who, beside early Depeche Mode fans, wants to pay money to watch a bunch of guys singing and hitting keyboards once in a while?

The answer these days is almost everybody under 35. Judging from the astounding ticket sales and blissed-out, cheering crowds, EDM shows are now the ultimate "live" music experience. Propulsive beats rattle your brain and rock your body, hyperactive light shows fry your eyes, and everybody is dancing, grooving, communing in that primal, groupthink buzz that comes with huge numbers of people doing something in unison. Resistance is futile. Skrillex and Afrojack shows resemble video games—with lights, lasers, and pyrotechnics. The shows are a celebration of sensory overload—the volcanic, body-shaking presence of the bass, rumbling and rocking you the entire evening. Girl Talk—a performer I'm told is now passé—offered a different, shambolic vibe. Girl Talk famously aimed to dissolve the separation of the audience and the artist by inviting revelers to party on stage, dancing and whooping. This is audience participation, but it also turns the audience into the performance. It's a fun idea. But Mr. Girl Talk doesn't create much music up there—he dances around, he looks at his two computers and mashes up fragments and riffs from classic rock with popular raps, usually over a thudding 4/4 beat, and then he rocks the party.

I'd concede Skrillex, Afrojack, and Girl Talk stage exciting "concerts"—except for the fact that none of them seem to be doing jack shit in terms of "playing" music, which is what makes—or used to make—a concert a concert. It might be more accurate to call EDM shows "performances." EDM artists and DJs don't even have a keyboard to hit, in most cases. There's just the ultra-boring click of a mouse—if that.

A pal of mine was in Prague. He was going up to his hotel room when EDM hero Paul Oakenfold walks into the elevator holding a metallic briefcase. "Is that where the magic happens?" my pal asks.

"This *is* the magic," says Paul, patting the briefcase.

Did he have a hard drive? A thumb drive? Music burned on discs? DATs? Who knows? The meaning was clear to my friend: He was not carrying his instrument; he was carrying the music itself.

The second reason I scoff has to do with EDM's rampant collaging and appropriation. Yes, some sampling can be ingenious. I get it. Recontextualization, as I pointed out while ranting about cover tunes, can be totally hypnotic and is to be applauded. But cloning hits, resplicing them, beefing them up, cutting-and-pasting, and then canning this work for a gig is, ultimately, the lowest rung on the performance creativity ladder. In fact, it's lamer than doing a straight cover, because *you are not even playing anything.*

In fact, there is an argument to be made that watching an EDM performance is essentially watching expensively choreographed karaoke. Someone is singing, or as is often the case, cheerleading, against a backing track.

Not caring about the performance of music is the ultimate consumer callousness. It doesn't matter who made it, or how it's made. It only matters when the listener wants to consume— listen to, dance to, play on their Beats. On some level, then, you might think EDM has the potential to exist on a higher plane, because it's all about the music. But that's not right either. Because it's not true. DJs have the same cults of personality that rock stars do, but it's not about chops, for the most part. It's about a sound and a brand.

I can hear some of you calling bullshit on me being uptight about appropriation—because so much of rock 'n' roll is based on appropriation, or as I like to call it: theft. And yes, this is true:

sampling is an act of audacity. It's like a micro-cover, rearranged and recontextualized. And anyway, the sound is the thing. The music either works or it doesn't. It moves you or it makes you yawn.

And those are good points. But just because technology makes it easy to be innovative or create does not make it impressive. Girl Talk and his by-the-numbers remixing on a Mac is fun pop art of the lowest point-and-click level. Skrillex deserves props for his singularly ridiculous haircut and his showmanship. Afrojack for his killer light show. Steve Aoki for some fearsome house-meets-video-game mixes. But musicianship and performance? I will not concede that an EDM DJ has the equivalent talent of a great guitarist, drummer, or singer. It is absurd to equate the non-songwriting, canned music DJ with a musical artist.

Ultimately, the frequently misnamed DJ is, at his or her highest creative point, a songwriter and a producer and an MC. And that is a worthy thing. But *musical* performance of the "artist"—an essential part of rock—is not a huge part of EDM. The lights, the sound system, the smart drinks, and drugs seem just as vital as a music-making DJ when it comes to live EDM performances, because the prerecorded music is played, but not made.

One of the magical ingredients of musical performance— why Jimi Hendrix and Jimmy Page and Johny Lydon and Mick Jagger are heroes and shamans—is the *thing*. They are virtuosos. Some master instruments, some sing. Some master attitude or stagecraft. But they all create in real time.

DJs? Sadly, many of them have to fist pump because they don't actually play anything, except, perhaps, the fans that shell out major bucks to see them.

Now get the hell off my lawn.

# WHAT WE WRITE ABOUT WHEN WE WRITE ABOUT ROCK, OR THE QUESTION OF ROCK CRITICISM

*THE WHOLE FAMILY IS IN THE CAR. WE'RE DRIVING AROUND BROOKLYN on Dekalb Street in Fort Greene. Stevie Wonder is on the car stereo. My son, in fourth grade at the time, calls from the back seat. "Who's more important: Stevie Wonder or Marvin Gaye?"*

*As I would do years later to discuss Billy Joel, I pull over and stop the car.*

*What a huge question. Even though my son grew up to defend his right to like Billy Joel, this inquiry was proof he was a genius at an early age.*

*"There is no easy answer," I say.*

*My wife is smiling. She gets it.*

*We sit there and we laugh, because we are so blown away by the fact our son even thought to pose this question. It shows he is thinking about music, that he is trying to place two great artists in some kind of context. Five years earlier, my son and I had discussed, like millions before us, who would win if Batman fought Superman. That was too easy. Obviously Superman would kick Batman's ass any day of the week, unless Batman got hold of some Kryptonite. Now he is asking for guidance about two Motown superheroes.*

*I search for an answer. On the face of it—given his hit singles—you might think Stevie would have this is a walk. But Marvin had, arguably, the first concept album in black pop. He wrote some incredibly sexy soul ballads. And he sang the national anthem a cappella at the 1983 NBA All-Star Game in Los Angeles, delivering one of the best versions of the song this side of Hendrix.*

*But then Stevie Wonder was a prodigy. A virtuoso! A wonder! His work in the '60s and '70s was unique and stunning and exploded into the world with dazzling speed. I adore the melodic sunshine of "My Cherie Amour," the walloping funk of "Higher Ground" and the dazzling-in-scope and execution of* Songs in the Key of Life.

*"It's like solving Fermat's theorem," I tell my 9-year-old son, although I'm really speaking to myself.*

*"He means it's a very hard to answer that question," my wife translates. "There is no right or wrong answer."*

*I think about saying "Hey, there must be a right answer, but I need some time here." Instead I shift into drive.*

*"Your mom's right," I say. "Back in the '70s Marvin was doing more socially daring things with his music. But he didn't really keep*

*that up, I don't think. Then Stevie got political with 'Living for the City' and 'You Haven't Done Nothin'.' But I think Marvin got there first. So that's something he has over Stevie Wonder."*

*"But Stevie Wonder is blind," my son says.*

*"So is your dad," my wife says. "Sometimes."*

DISCUSSING MUSIC AMONG FAMILY AND FRIENDS IS ONE OF MY favorite activities. So is reading about it. I became aware of rock writing, in fact, during an exchange with my father. This was in 1977 or just after, and I must have been about 13 years old. My dad had brought a cheapo Yardbirds compilation album. The album featured early tracks by Eric Clapton, Jeff Beck, and Jimmy Page, three guitarists who had all played for the Yardbirds. I'm pretty sure the marquee names and the Yardbirds connection and bargain LP price were why he bought the album, because I remember him putting the platter on the turntable and saying: "I once saw the Yardbirds."

Then he laughed. "I covered a concert. I think it might have been the worst music review in history. I remember writing that people seemed to like it and were clapping enthusiastically."

My dad—Michael T. Kaufman was his *New York Times* byline, but he was Mike to his friends—had no musical training. He was proud of his whistling skills and he liked to sing hokey old songs with my mom in the car. He was the one who brought Beatles and Dylan and Rolling Stones records to our home in the '60s. And the *Woodstock* and the *Concert for Bangladesh* albums in the '70s. He even covered Woodstock as a reporter, flying in by helicopter because the roads were closed. But the fact was, in 1967, when the Yardbirds came to town, he didn't have any experience with rock writing because rock writing didn't really exist. Yes, there were music magazines. *Billboard*, which started back in the late 1800s covering the market for posters, had morphed into a music industry trade magazine. And in the U.K., *Melody Maker* and *New Musical Express* had been around for decades, serving musicians not fans. I'm sure there were fanzines and regional coverage of rock, and *Crawdaddy,* the first "serious" music mag, started publishing sporadically in 1966. But *Rolling Stone* magazine didn't start until 1967. So covering rock was still new terrain when my dad went to hear Jimmy Page tear it up.

Recently, I hunted down the *Times* article my dad had laughed about. "Yardbirds Complete 6th Mission to Expand Young Minds in the U.S.," trumpets the headline found on page 36 of the August 28, 1967, paper, sandwiched between ads for *To Sir, With Love* and Sandy Dennis in *Up the Down Staircase,* and an article titled, "Alpert Concert Defies the Rain." Read in hindsight, it's quaint and amusing by modern standards, but I came away thinking my dad was a tough critic—of himself.

For one thing, it's as much a profile and news story as it is a review, which isn't that surprising considering my dad was a general assignment reporter at the time. It's more about the Yardbirds in America circa 1967 than about the Yardbirds' musical performance, per se. Here's the lede:

*The Yardbirds, four soft-spoken hard-playing Englishmen, ended their sixth money-making tour of the U.S. this weekend by "doing their thing" loudly and enthusiastically at an East Village concert.*

So you can see my dad's embarrassment, right? *Enthusiastically?* Isn't that a given for most bands? Even ultra grim punks and metalists put on a show. And *money-making*? You have to wonder where that came from. Did the manager stress that? The record company publicist? Did touring bands usually not make money? Meanwhile, *"doing their thing"*— which doesn't really explain what the "thing" is—worked as wordplay, a contemporary joke using the hip slang of the moment. Let's go on:

*The quartet, a major contributor to the sonic boom shaking both sides of the Atlantic Ocean, attracted a diverse audience of youths—unkempt, barefoot, kempt and shod—with their driving, often improvisational playing.*

My dad the reporter was "doing his thing" here: giving us color and context. But he clearly lacked the precise music vocabulary—the British Invasion or blues revival—of the day. But we get it. And he even gets a laugh with his description of the crowd: *unkempt, barefoot, kempt and shod.*

And then, Mike Kaufman, reporter, transgresses what is now an unwritten rule of criticism. He *talks* to the band after the gig! I love two things about this. First, it provides evidence my dad once hung out backstage with Jimmy Page! How cool is that? Second, when does a reviewer or critic ever hang out with a band after a gig? That's the stuff of profiles, of magazine pieces, of interviews. The unwritten rules of newspaper music criticism are nowhere in sight in this piece. Instead, color and wit replace musical analysis and context. Which is to say, nowhere does my dad mention the Yardbirds' million-selling hit, "For Your Love," or their raucous riffing "Heart Full of Soul," or Page's famous guitar-slinging predecessors Clapton and Beck. For all I know, at the time my dad, who died in 2010, may not have been aware of those songs or that Eric Clapton and Jeff Beck were former band members. In 1967 he was trying to work his way up the *NY Times* ladder, and helping raise me, my brother, and our five-month-old sister. It seems entirely possible the Yardbirds were off his radar.

Back to the article: *The drummer, Jim McCarty, went out to smoke (tobacco) with his girlfriend.* The stoner humor comes back again quoting Keith Relf, who talks about expanding the audience's mind. *"We hope we still do that, but we don't have to rely on drugs."*

*But then, catching himself in what might be thought a minor heresy, he added, "Don't get the wrong idea, we're not anti-pot."*

In the end, I think my dad was too harsh on himself. This is not the worst concert review ever written. It's actually pretty damn cool for the 1967 *New York Times*. It's a time capsule, a tiny entry in the evolution of rock writing.

And that evolution is striking. We have a nation of middle-of-the-road reviewers, critics who think their job is to deliver "service" reviews. We have apologists, feminists, semioticians, popsters.

I went on the Internet to look for the album my dad had purchased all those years ago. I couldn't actually remember the title, but for some reason—amazing what strange details get filed in your brain—I remembered the label name: Pickwick. I searched "Yardbirds Pickwick" and eventually spotted a familiar-looking, garish, multicolored '70s album cover depicting three long-haired guitarists. It was called "Guitar Boogie" and I had, as George Bush might put it, mis-remembered: It wasn't actually a Yardbirds album, it was a 1977 reissue of studio recordings of Clapton, Beck, and Page. And some of the tracks had Clapton and Page playing together.

# METAPHYSICAL GRAFFITI

As I was searching for this obscure album, I found pictures of the front and back cover, and I discovered the liner notes were written by rock criticism founding father Richard Meltzer, who helped "invent" the form around the time my dad wrote his Yardbirds review. As I noted earlier, Meltzer published a book, *The Aesthetics of Rock*.

I must have read his liner notes to *Guitar Boogie* as a 13-year-old, and rereading them decades later, they felt familiar—but not in an instantly good way. I remembered I never "got" many Meltzer pieces I've read over the years. And, to be honest, I never really "got" the band he helped form, Blue Oyster Cult, which, aside from "(Don't Fear) The Reaper," left me cold. Even the hit Meltzer wrote—"I'm Burnin' for You"—struck me as lame 80s rock.

But whatever. The liner notes on *Guitar Boogie* are dizzying—full of jokes and insider references to Clapton's love life and Jimmy Page's genteel lifestyle, without much explanation. If you aren't steeped in the blues and rock—and even if you are—you have to decode his writing.

And maybe that was part of the point, to be a smart smartass. But that comes with a price. Too much criticism—literary, rock, art, movies—is disengaging, and the reasons for this span the entire form. Service-oriented criticism, while noble, is often bland and at its blandest, arguably, it isn't criticism at all. You know the drill: "This sounds like this and is different from the last record and has these new or old influences." This is fine. But it's pretty boring. It doesn't really excite the way a song can. Not the way a really innovative or outrageous review or think piece can engage.

Which brings us to academic reviews. I'm a grad school dropout, and while I really liked some of the criticism I read— yes, at times I found criticism *exciting*, I admit it—there were also dense, coded pieces that were DEATHLY boring. They were the opposite of rock. Well, the opposite of *good* rock: turgid, pretentious, long-winded, inaccessible, and utterly without swing or funk. Unlike comprehensible service pieces, academic reviews require readers have knowledge of critical frameworks— semiotics, hermeneutics, deconstruction—and the vast body of work that has gone before, in order to understand the critique.

But music criticism can be fun and accessible and creative. It can swing. It can solo. It can rock. And it doesn't require degrees in music, literary criticism, or philosophy—although no doubt they can be useful. And while Meltzer is sometimes unreadable and sophomoric (the guy plays in a band called Smegma, which is the word for scummy secretions under the foreskin), I like the man in theory. At least he was having fun. He was clearly passionate, knowledgeable, obsessive, and CREATIVE. Unfortunately, he sometimes risked losing the reader. I'm sure I've been guilty of the same thing.

Reading Meltzer's *The Aesthetics of Rock*, which he disavows in the preface to a later edition of the book—while urging readers, in true hype-rock fashion, to buy his *other* books—can be headache inducing. But wading through the jump cut-filled treatise, you get the sense that criticism is more than analysis and more than just deconstructing a song—the instruments, the words, the notes. It's about making connections, about providing context, about transforming or translating its impact onto the page. It's a continuum and feedback loop: You listen, you watch, you feel, you dance, you write, you share.

Which brings me to Lester Bangs.

When it comes to sharing and being creative, Bangs is my favorite rock writer. Rarely has anyone come close to the anarchy, comedy, and biography that Bangs conjured up. Not that he's perfect. He goes on too long, sometimes his riffs drift. But a man who goes on stage and bangs on a typewriter while the J. Geils Band plays "Give It to Me," and then destroys his Smith-Corona, à la the Who, isn't just a critic. He's an artist. He's one of the guys who understands criticism is an art, a way to express yourself and tell stories about music, musicians, yourself, and the world.

And just like a song can hook or lose readers, rock writing can, too. Bangs' classic book, *Psychotic Reactions and Carburetor Dung*—a collection that finds him recalling first crushes, fantasizing about killing James Taylor, getting under Lou Reed's skin—kicks out the jams and liberates criticism, thanks to its gonzo improvisational and confessional riffs. Rereading it, I imagine Bangs teaching a class in rock writing, shouting: "Criticism is a performance, people! It's a party!" I like to think he'd say: "NEVER bore your audience! If it doesn't rock for you, how is it going to rock your reader?"

David Lee Roth once said, "Most rock critics like Elvis Costello because most rock critics look like Elvis Costello." Well, sadly most rock critics don't write like Lester Bangs, and too many write like they never heard of the guy. That's a tragedy, especially in this day and age of easy publishing. Where are the autobiographical gonzo tales that explain the Pink Floyd bastard child that is Radiohead? Or the ecstatic—and yes, I mean drug-addled—defenses of EDM "concerts" as the modern-day equivalent of a religious revival show? Or the obvious takedown of *Hamilton*'s outrageously priced ticket sales from scalpers as the apotheosis of the title character's protectionist-shaped investment market beliefs?[11] Yeah, I know: being found on Google means you need keyword density; that's more important than a rambling, joyful, inventive 20,000-word rethink of the Troggs that imagines murder, sex, and the birth of punk before punk was even birthed.

There are practically no rock magazines in America anymore. But there is the web and thousands of websites. And they may not pay or pay much, but then almost nobody has ever gotten rich writing about music, just like the vast majority of bands have never made a penny playing music. Musicians did it for the sex and drugs, goes the old, cynical saw. Writers? We did it for … why do we do it?

The best music writers I've encountered have had good ears, imagination, and a missionary zeal. They introduced me to new sounds and ideas, writing about music with enthusiasm and knowledge. And quite often, they made me laugh, or think, or hate.[12] And they improved my musical knowledge exponentially. Fanzines turned me on to dozens of bands pre-internet, as did *The Village Voice*. *The Voice's* pop music editor, Robert Christgau, who certainly looked more like Elvis Costello than David Lee Roth,

---

11 For the record, I am a big Federalism fan. I'm just sayin' somebody should be sayin' it's fitting yet sad the man who issued America's first government-backed bonds inspired a musical in which speculative scalpers are charging and making disgusting amounts of money.

12 Who are these inspirations? The list is long and incomplete. Zine writers like Gerald Cosloy, Byron Coley, Mike Ruben, and the contributors of the short-lived *Swellsville*. The wizards I first read in *The Village Voice*: the hilarious macho Chuck Eddy, quip-master-turned-heartstring-puller Rob Sheffield, and eggheads Robert Christgau and Greil Marcus. I'm also grateful for *Times* scribes Robert Palmer and Jon Pareles.

handed out grades and sociocultural quips with his consumer guide of capsule reviews. But I'd trade all his pithy paragraphs for a quarterly version of his annual critics poll roundup, which tried to tell us what popular music was saying about the times we live in, and what the critics were saying about the times we lived in. Who does this now? Where are the synthesists who can decode and impart insightful and entertaining cultural criticism? Am I lost and out of touch? There are tremendous music websites out there—Aquarium Drunkard, Brooklyn Vegan, Awesome Tapes from Africa, and Dangerous Minds. But most of these sites report and discover or rediscover. Big ideas? Cultural interpretation? Gonzo criticism? Sometimes Pitchfork and Vice go there. But not enough.

When I think about this, I think, shit, let's exhume and clone Lester Bangs. Somebody launch a site that doesn't give a shit about word count or keyword density or traffic. Let's put it out there. Let's have personality. Let's be subjective. Let passion rule, because, fuck it—taste, aesthetics, identity, authenticity— it's all a giant jumble, and what makes sense to me may not make sense to you, and that's okay. Just sit on the couch and tell me about it.

Criticism. It's not just performance, it's a form of therapy.

SPEAKING OF THERAPY, I RECENTLY SPENT A WEEKEND WITH some old friends from college. Depending on your perspective, it was an annual, family-friendly celebration, or a midlife crisis support group. Or both. As my pals' kids played hide-and-seek in an old barn, we spent hours discussing music, jamming, recalling great concerts we had seen, wondering if we were missing out on new music, or if there is anything left to be said about the Beatles (I said yes, a Deadhead friend said no). Some of the concerts people shared didn't sound very enticing to me—Black Sabbath, with its slow metal plod, is a band I never "got." But that's okay, I was interested in hearing about it. And I even hung in there when people started recalling Grateful Dead shows. Generally, I listened happily, and started thinking about my own favorite shows: accidentally seeing a weirdo band called Devo when I was 13. James Blood Ulmer killing it on guitar on a boat in the Hudson River with about 10 people on board. Showing up in Amsterdam for one night and catching the Bembeya Jazz National at the Milky Way. The Stones at Shea Stadium from about 30 yards away. The New York debut of the obscure but excellent Kitchens of Distinction. My own gigs opening for bands I admired—Tom Tom Club, Yo La Tengo, the Feelies, and 10,000 Maniacs. Seeing Dream Syndicate's Paul Cutler use a power drill as a high-voltage slide guitar, the bit whirling against the strings.

And then, at night, four of my pals plugged their laptops and memory sticks into a big sound system, sat at a table, and took turns spinning—if that's still the word for it—tunes until 4 a.m.

At this point in my life, I often talk about and read about music more than I listen to it. But that's often been the case. My dad was eventually made a foreign correspondent for the *Times*, I grew up overseas, which meant that I frequently read about rock music long before I heard it. Now, with millions and millions of songs available on the internet, it is possible to listen to and discover new and different music with minimal effort; Spotify, Pandora, and other subscription services will even find them for you based on the previous songs you've listened to. But I grew up listening to shortwave radio, slowly spinning the radio dial in search of new music and waiting—praying—that DJs would tell me what I was listening to. I was so curious and thirsty to know about new music, I'd even skim the capsule reviews of outdated issues of *People* magazine at my school library. That's hunger.

Call and response may be the oldest musical structure in human history. A singer—say, Ronnie Isley in the song "Shout"—sings "Ay-ay-ay-ay!" And his band or the audience responds, repeating the phrase: "Ay-ay-ay-ay!" Talking about music is another response to the call of music. So is dancing. So is clapping or laughing or cheering or playing air guitar or flicking your BIC lighter, or more likely activating your glowing cell phone, and waving it above your head.

And so is writing about it.

Unfortunately, writing about music rarely has the instant gratification that playing or listening to music has. But writing about music is, at a basic level, a creative response. Just like dancing, but rarely as sexy or fun. It's an attempt to decode the music, to interpret it, remember it, scorn it, to testify to it. And the best music writing is creative and distinctive, enlightening and entertaining. Writers have voices just like musicians. Oh, to write criticism as cutting and memorable as John Lydon's fresh work with the Sex Pistols and PiL, or as mystical and moving as Nick Drake.

I have never understood the knee-jerk anti-intellectual response that some people have to music criticism. "Who cares?" scoff the people who don't care. "This is like Batman vs. Superman," scorn others who dismiss the Beatles or Stones question.

To me, music writing is glorious information and opinion. It's an act of transcription, of someone sharing their personal act of hearing, of being in their head and trying to share sound, or interpret sound. Sharing meaning … that is a great pursuit. Because music is communal. And so is writing about rock.

You get to respond, like all readers. You get to say, Kaufman is a shithead, a windbag! The guy's got no taste, no logic, and he's deaf and a total snob who doesn't like Billy Joel or *Glee*! Good!

Or maybe you laughed at something on these pages. Good! Or maybe you thought that's a good point, or that's ripped from the pages of *The Captain Obvious Guide to Music*!

Putting music under a microscope and examining it extends the groove for everyone. Attempting to explain the magic of sound and of hearing, that miracle, that moment when vibrations hit our ears, hit our brains like some drug, some art, some artdrug that makes us feel, that makes us remember other music and other times, places and people—the things that make up who we were and who we are and who and what we want to be—because, hey, this is serious. This is rock 'n' roll. Think about music. Humans have created sound waves that appeared and disappeared for 200,000 years, transmitted person to person, generation to generation. Then music became encoded, and could exist as notes on paper. A few hundred years later it was encoded in vinyl, on magnetic tape or digitally. Now it's everywhere. It's fucking universal!

Or is it?

Our experiences are not the same. Our tastes and upbringing and aesthetic rules are all different. You may (misguidedly) adore Billy Joel. You may even like having sex while listening to Rush. What we talk about when we talk about rock is an accounting of our lives, our selves, our values, the relation of music to all of those things, and the power, the effect, music has over us. Yes, I can pull the song out of context. I can examine the sonic components, break down the structure, analyze the text, dissect the market, and track the inspiration, the influences, and the motives of the songwriters. All of that is legit, especially if you wasted three years building debt in grad school to learn how to do it, and it adds to the discussion.

Buddhist philosopher Alan Watts noted English speakers use the verb "play" to describe the act of making music. That is to say, musicians "play" a song when they perform it. And music fans "play" a recording of a song when they want to hear it. This is a wonderful, perfectly fitting linguistic usage. Yes, music can be a chore: Listening to Kenny G or Journey can be the opposite of play, but you know what I mean. Music is fun. And rock 'n' roll is really fun! Performing it, listening to it, dancing to it, is all fun, all play.

But play—as in kids playing with blocks or dressing up—has other meanings, and it should be noted that, as reams of educational research tell us, it can be a learning experience, too, one that is critical to developing problem-solving skills, social skills, motor skills, and more.

Every time you listen to music it can be an act of worship or discovery or play. Or something you take for granted, like air. The decoding and sharing of music—essentially playing with it—brings us closer to each other and to the music itself. And if we stop to think about it, it can be overwhelming. Why does this power, this force—which persists *in every single society*—exist?

What we do when we write about music—whether sharing, reviewing, fantasizing, interpreting, contextualizing—is actively celebrate that awesome power and the power we get from it. The power that forces us to ask questions, to create a different kind of music—a kind of music about music.

A different kind of play.

# ACKNOWLEDGMENTS

Many people helped shape this book and my listening skills or lack thereof. Thanks to:

Robert Jourdain, whose *Music, the Brain and Ecstasy* is a must-read for anyone exploring the science behind our love of music.

Stephen Mumford, whose *Metaphysics* primer helped me solve air guitar conundrums.

Designer Kevin McLaughlin for a great cover, Sarah Masterson Hally for awesome interior design, and Gerry Putzer for eagle-eyed copy editing.

The insightful and delightful team at OR Books who helped get this book off the ground: Colin Robinson, John Oakes. Emily Freyer, Emma Ingrisani, Alex Doherty, and Shuja Haider.

Early readers: Marc Catapano, Ray St. Dennis, Markus Hoffman, Gary Marmmorstein, Sarah Morris, Jamie Pallot, Chris Parker, and Mark Schwartz.

My mom, Rebecca, who patiently underwrote guitar lessons when I was 8, 10, and 12—even though I quit each time.

The people who have helped me hear better: Daniel Blackman, Doug Foote, David Gresalfi, Andrew Hook, Barbara Lerner, Bill Lambertson, Chris Mandros, Gerry Mullany, Gerard O'Brien, Mitch Rosen, Dan Roth, Mark Schwartz, Lydia Vanderloo, Seth Walter, and WHRW and WFMU DJs.

And, finally, the trio that endures and instructs while I process new sounds and ideas—Theo Kaufman, Hilary Kaufman, and Susan Pottinger.